*The
Working
Mother*

SIDNEY CORNELIA CALLAHAN

The
Working
Mother

THE MACMILLAN COMPANY, NEW YORK, NEW YORK
COLLIER-MACMILLAN LIMITED, LONDON

Acknowledgments

I would like to thank the sixteen women who gave me so much of their time and effort. Their honesty in self-appraisal was refreshing. I would also like to thank those dedicated professors at Sarah Lawrence College who enlarged my understanding of child development. These particular people contributed most specifically to this book; but in addition, there have been countless others who have discussed the working mother's problems with me by the hour. Reading the literature in the field prepares one academically to discuss this question, but I really owe this book to the women I have known.

To my husband, Daniel, and our children,
Mark, Stephen, John, Peter, Sarah and David.

Contents

The
Working
Mother

1

It's All Right to Want to Work

The 1970s may be remembered in future eras as the decade of the great feminine revolt. Not since the suffragette movement have so many women been aroused and concerned for their own welfare as a group. Women are making new demands and creating new life styles far different from those of the stereotyped women who were bound to church, kitchen, and children.

Although the number of women actually involved in women's liberation groups may be small, many more women are quietly cheering their more radical sisters on. Many other women agree with some of the feminists' demands but not all of them. Finally, there are the women who are untouched as yet by the ferment. But these women too will soon be affected, in a country in which the newspapers and television relay everything to everybody with amazing speed. One way or another, no adult woman or any young woman now coming into adulthood is going to avoid a reappraisal of women's changing role in American society.

In this great revolt the focus will not be on voting and civil rights. Women still do not have full equality under the law, but they are close enough to having formal legal equality. The remaining obstacle for women and their rallying cause this time centers on the informal structures of our society—those beliefs, expectations, and customs which govern group life beyond the law. In this more private realm, the relationships within the family are crucial in shaping women's work and self-image.

In other words, while the law may guarantee that women are equal with their husbands before the law, custom may still govern the marriage relationship and insure that the husband is dominant. Similarly, while all professions and jobs may be legally open to women, custom may subtly, or not so subtly, arrange it so that the top positions go to men only. Women may be kept from certain kinds of work and persuaded toward other work solely on the basis of their femininity. Talent will not count. Traditionally, women's work has included the rearing of the children, housework, and jobs which are closely allied to these occupations. While both parents in a family are legally responsible for their children, the mother has been given the major responsibility and all of the child care.

Women today are challenging all of these customary assumptions about women's work and women's role in the family and society. Along with other minority groups they cry: Let legal equality be followed by social equality. Let women expand their work roles and expectations. Let us reorganize the family and society to liberate women. Whatever it takes to effect true women's liberation in consciousness and in fact, let's do it now.

At this point in the argument, of course, people begin to differ over what it takes. Finding good ways to change society is harder than simply realizing that things are unfair as they are. Not only do people differ on methods, but there are wide differences in the goals being sought under the common name of women's liberation. Getting a consensus on goals is a prerequisite for effective organization and leadership. There are many complicated questions about the nature of work and the organization of family life which need to be thought through carefully.

The most complicating factor in the question of woman's liberation has to do with the beginning of another revolution which should be called the children's liberation movement. The new awareness that women are subtly oppressed in our culture has also produced a new understanding of what a child needs. We understand at last that children do not just grow. They need a great deal of care and stimulation in order to fulfill their intellectual and social potential. Much of the research which has been done on the early child's capacities and the older child's needs has brought home to many concerned child experts just how grievously we fail our children. Thus we witness the slow, quiet beginnings of the children's liberation movement, working against the false myth that America is a child-centered society.

In this time of change and crisis, then, we have the beginnings of two freedom movements. The inevitable question follows: Do the interests of women and the interests of children conflict? Not nearly enough people address themselves to this problem. The child experts and the women's liberation supporters are rarely one and the same. Child development specialists see things from the viewpoint of the child and his needs. Women's lib people tend to look at things from the individual woman's point of view, often seeing children and child care as the main obstacle to women's taking a truly equal place in the world.

Again, child-care experts usually wish to strengthen the family, assuming that a strong family helps the development of the child. Many women in the women's liberation movement, however, wish to downgrade the importance of marriage and the family. Many radical feminists insist that marriage and family always end in the oppression and suppression of women. Even the more moderate groups who push for child-care centers, make it quite clear that these measures are primarily for freeing women *from* children and not primarily *for* children.

Those people in the child-care movement who also advocate day care usually do so as a compensatory measure. Since so many of our families are strained and broken, day-care centers are seen as necessary supplements to depleted families, rather than the best solution arrived at in the best of all possible worlds. People working in the ghettoes of the city or in other pockets of poverty worry over the fragility of the family, especially when there is an absent father. Feminists may be complaining about the father's career coming first, and worrying about how this suppresses opportunities for the wife; but in some subcultures in our country, the traditional male-dominated, two-parent family would be an improvement. An intact family with a male head of the household helps the development of the children, especially the development of boys.

Can all of these conflicts of interest be reconciled? Can the child experts, the women's liberation people, and the family get together? I think they can. I think our solution lies in transforming our idea and ideal of work, along with our ideal of family. If we can understand the importance and the human need for work and can gain a new ideal of the extended family freely recreated, then we can restructure our society creatively rather than destructively. With the proper safeguards for everyone's unique situation, we can create social solutions in which men, women, and children can be liberated together. No one should pay a price for another's fulfillment, especially when its our children.

Following a discussion of this solution and the insights and transformations needed, here are sixteen concrete experiences of women living today in America who combine work and child rearing, with varying degrees of support and nonsupport from those around them. Their experiences point up the achievements and the inadequacies of our present society. We learn as much, if not more, from our failures and problems as from successes. None of these women is part of the radical new movement for women's liberation; they struggled or sailed through their experiences well before the seventies. Not being in the radical avant-garde, their experiences are all the more meaningful for other women facing these same challenges and conflicts. Most women are still going to marry and have children, and will have to work out their own individual solutions. The diversity of approach and experience among these women is encouraging.

The one great common denominator in all of these women's lives was their concern for their children and their feeling about the value of work. The most central question I put to them on my questionnaire (*see* Appendix) was, "Why do you work?" This is a question that all self-conscious adults must answer for themselves at one time or another. But women in our culture who work outside the home have often had to answer this as a question charged with aggression. Among many people the assumption was made that if you wanted to work it was a sign that something was wrong with you as a woman.

A classic statement of this earlier view can be found in an 1889 publication called *The Forum*. Grant Allen, a well-known scientific popularizer of the day laid it down in no uncertain terms: "All that is distinctly human is man; the field, the ship, the mine, the work-shop; all that is truly woman is merely reproductive—the nursery, the schoolroom. There are women to be sure who inherit much of male faculty; and some of these prefer to follow male vocations; but in so doing they for the most part unsex themselves; they fail to perform satisfactorily their maternal duties."[1] Here we see the either/or decision absolutely entrenched, either you are feminine and stick to the truly womanly endeavors of reproduction, or you unsex yourself and follow male vocations, insuring maternal failure to boot.

We might be able to laugh at such either/or dichotomies today if they had not been reinforced by a much more modern and subtle doctrine which wafted over our world from 19th-century Vienna. The great Freudian tidal wave inundated our culture in the 1940s and '50s and took its toll. In psychoanalysis, Freud's dictum that "anatomy is destiny" spelled bad news for women. Among the orthodox, the feminine core involved a harmonious blend of masochism, narcissism, and passivity. To be fulfilled sexually and maternally was woman's most important goal. Any women or revisionist psychoanalysts who asserted that women's striving for work outside the home might not be compensatory feminine protest was dismissed. Everyone understood that while women's "penis envy" might make problems in properly adjusting to their fem-

[1] Quoted in Robert W. Smuts, *Women and Work in America* (New York: Columbia University Press, 1959), p. 116.

inine role, truly feminine women would not aspire to masculine work and life styles.

In the midst of so much "pop" Freudianism, earlier feminist gains in securing the vote and the right to be educated got swamped by the belief that sexuality is all-determining. The sexual mystique became "the feminine mystique," which has been so well chronicled. The differences between men and women were emphasized and the sexual component in personality was not considered a component, but all-encompassing. Since women were women, they needed to be related to a man and to be maternally fulfilled. Marriage and childbearing were the highest functions to which women could aspire. If women did work outside the home, they should try to find suitably feminine vocations and not be aggressive or overly concerned with their work.

Women who were not totally fulfilled in marriage and childbearing were made to feel that something was wrong with them. Why did they want to work, when just by being wives and mothers they shoud be fulfilled? Big families were also the fashion in the '50s and the beginning of the resurgence in arts and crafts made the feminine role seem a full one for many women. Women were believed to have very different satisfactions and roles than men would, or could, aspire to. Somehow the sexual hormones and all the somatic factors in feminine and masculine identities were thought to be inundating all of the personality, including the brain. Any work that would be done would be directly related to sexual personality. So there had to be woman's work and man's work, with little overlap. Men were aggressive, abstract thinkers and doers, and women were nurturers and passive receivers. The two sexes were complementary to each other through their distinct sexual differences.

Fortunately, this combined Freudian-folk-wisdom orthodoxy began to be questioned on all sides during the '60s.
Women attacked the sexual mystique most vigorously and
cited in their defense the findings of sociology and an-
thropology. These new social sciences were discovering
the influence of social conditioning; in so doing they were
questioning the all-determining character of sexual identity with its supposedly innate characteristics built into
maleness and femaleness. The new and disturbing question arising from cross-cultural studies was: If other cultures start from the same biological base and elaborate
very different structures for the woman's role, why must
our difference and subordination be innately determined?

Man the culture-maker was rediscovered by feminists.
The older biologism comparing man to the animals did
not grant enough uniqueness to man, who as a species
shapes himself through culture. Women are made, as
much as they are born. Feminists like Simone de Beauvoir
and Betty Friedan made this point very strongly in the
last decade, and it doesn't have to be reargued at this late
date. We know how much culture and environment shape
our development; but it is not so well known that even
in individual personality theory there has been a drastic
reassessment of human development.

The great revolution here is the discovery of the importance of cognitive development. Somehow in the great
Freudian breakthrough man's rationality got slighted;
understandably so, since Freud was trying to force an un-
willing scientific community to realize that there was an
irrational side of man. Fifty years after Freud, the big
breakthroughs and most exciting developments revolve
around discoveries of how human beings learn to think
and reason. So much more is going on in a developing
human being than Freud could account for with his rudi-

mentary theory of the ego. Though he revised his thinking all of his life, the great revisions and changes in ego
psychology were left to his followers.

The realization of the importance of the ego, of making
rational decisions and coping with reality, is tremendously significant for both women's and children's liberation. The point is that women and children have egos
which need satisfaction and stimulation. The ego, too,
strives to do its own thing. Egos are not enslaved to or
energized by the drives and instincts, but have a development all of their own. As Heinz Hartmann, one of the
founders of ego psychology, expressed it, in addition to
drives and instincts, human development includes "perception, intention, object comprehension, thinking, language, recall phenomena, productivity . . . motor development . . . and the maturation and learning processes im-
plicit in all of these and many others." [2]

These capacities and developments in the ego are
serving independent biological functions and make the
individual capable of adapting to reality. Reality here
includes one's self as well as the external environment. All
of these ego processes are as important as the drives and
sexual components of the personality. They are, in revised ego psychology, independent and do not arise from
conflicts in the instinctual sphere. Thus, when men, women
and children are thinking and doing, their activity does
not arise from some sexual frustration or conflict. Thinking is not just a defense against sexual anxiety, or a substitute sexual satisfaction, but something primary that
human beings do by virtue of being human.

No one much questions this in regard to men, who
can think, work, shape, and do without suspicion. How-

[2] Heinz Hartmann, *Ego Psychology and the Problem of Adaptation* (New York: International Universities Press, 1958), p. 8.

ever, in the case of women, it is liberating to understand
that thinking is natural to them too, and not a sign of
sexual frustration. The rise of ego psychology has started
to break down the either/or bind. One is not either sexy
or smart, because one can be sexy *and* smart. Sexual and
emotional developments are one important process, and
ego development with the capacity to think, do, and act
is another important process. One is not necessarily developed at the expense of the other. A woman's highly developed ego does not mean that her sexual and maternal
motivations will be less developed.

In the independent development of a human ego, sexual drives interact with innate curiosity. Motivation studies have also been recently revolutionized. A strong, independent motivation toward activity, exploration, and
change exists even in animals such as rats and monkeys.
Well-fed and well-watered monkeys will work without
extrinsic reward at taking apart a six-device puzzle for ten
hours and more. Rats will cross electrified barriers to explore new territories, or press bars in boxes in order to
provoke stimulus change. Knowing this about animals,
it is all the less surprising to find that human beings also
seek activity and thrive on novelty, just for its own, sweet
sake.

Being alive means being active. A newborn baby already has continually active brain cells ready and waiting
to be matched by experience. From the beginning of life,
the human organism craves the right amount of stimulation. Evidently, as a species, we also have strong spontaneous motivations to explore, to seek change, to manipulate,
to organize, and to do. Change, complexity, novelty, activity, patterning, and mastering are instrinsically self-
rewarding. Babies will choose to look at a more complex
stimulus figure rather than be bored by simpler and

already mastered pictures. The small scientist in his crib is busy from birth on, observing and figuring out the world through his experiments. We are born ready and willing to work on the world and enjoy every minute of it.

When the human being does not have stimulating work or activity and must lie in enforced passivity, all sorts of dire things happen. Spontaneously motivated to do and act and seek challenge, bored human beings truly suffer. Babies may be literally bored to death or into mental retardation in cold, unstimulating institutions. We also know what happens to college students in an experiment with the pathology of boredom. When you put people in padded suits in darkened rooms, removing all possibility of movement, noise, light, etc., no one of them can be paid enough to tolerate the unpleasant experience for more than a few days. Even with all of their instinctual needs satisfied, an overwhelming desire for variation develops, often resulting in restlessness, mental disorganization and hallucinations.[3] Obviously, it is torture to be isolated with too little stimulation and no activity. Even with all somatic needs taken care of, the ego and the brain can hunger and thirst. Women and children are no exception to this basic human need for novel stimulation and appropriate challenges.

Apparently there is in our species a basic drive and delight in competence and patterned doing. R. W. White, the psychologist, has written that competence or a feeling of "effectance" in transactions with the environment yields pleasure.[4] Needing to learn as much as we do to

---

[3] Wilbert James McKeachie and Charlotte Lackner Doyle, *Psychology* (Reading, Mass.: Addison-Wesley Publishing Co., 1966), Chapter 7, "Motivation," pp. 216-254.

[4] R. W. White, "Motivation Reconsidered: The Concept of Competence," *Psychological Review*, 66 (1959), pp. 297-333.

survive, it is logical that the species enjoys interacting with the environment and gets a moderate pleasure from this activity. Shaping of self and environment, figuring out the world, and organizing it (call it work) are basically enjoyable. Man works not only because work is adaptive for survival but because work gives pleasure. Once immediate needs for survival have been met, and food and safety are no longer a problem, then man will be motivated by competence or self-actualizing motives. Viscerogenic needs will naturally give way to psychogenic needs in most hierarchies of human motivation. Once you have bread, you no longer live by bread alone.

One very strong need of the developing ego is to develop a particular competence in one's own culture which can focus the general urge toward effectance common to the species. Erik Erikson maintains in his theory of ego development that this is a need manifested in all human cultures. Both boys and girls need to develop this particular form of competence which he defines in this way: "Competence, then, is the free exercise of dexterity and intelligence and the completion of tasks, unimpaired by infantile inferiority. It is the basis for cooperative participation in technologies and relies, in turn, on the logic of tools and skills." [5] Competence is an intersexual virtue which the ego must develop on the road to adult identity and integrity.

Such an exercise of reasonableness and workmanship gives a personality a salutory self-verification as he or she cooperates with others in obtaining goals which the culture values. In our recent American culture neither women nor children have been allowed to develop or exercise competence. It mainly has been the prerogative of the

[5] Erik Erikson, *Insight and Responsibility* (New York: W. W. Norton, 1964), p. 129.

adult male, since most of the work of the world moved out of the home, leaving the women and children behind. Schools, segregated from where the action is, and good housekeeping in the suburbs have not always activated "the free exercise of intelligence," or "the logic of tools and skills."

Women have missed out lately on "the cooperative participation in technologies," and in that most important aspect of competence, "the completion of tasks." In rural frontier America, maintaining a home and farm entailed participation in a logic of skills and tools along with other adult workers in the household. Moreover, the seasonal organization of life gave some sense of completion. *The* fall harvesting, *the* summer canning, *the* spring planting, or housecleaning were major enterprises which stayed done for a year. Whatever a woman did, it was absolutely necessary for the survival and well-being of her family. She had little choice or time for brooding over work fulfillment.

Today, in the middle-class home filled with appliances there is no fixed seasonal routine nor sense of absolute necessity. At the same time standards of cleanliness and cuisine are phenomenally high. Thus, with washer and drier, vacuum cleaner and waxers, there is a succession of unending and relatively undemanding tasks. Affluent domestic housework tends to be fragmented, unspecialized, interrupted, and unstructured. There is no nine-to-five structure and the unceasing nature of the work does not demand major effort or give major satisfaction from completion of tasks.

A survey of the comparative time spent on housework by rural housewives and city women revealed that while rural women spent sixty hours a week housekeeping, city women spent eighty hours. The compilers of the report, who do not seem to have heard of Parkinson's Law, were puzzled and said so. "Contrary to commonsense expectations, as living standards grow higher and more appliances and services enter the home, women tend to spend more time on home activity." [6]

In urbanized, industrialized homes, many women find themselves spending more time on less demanding activity in greater isolation from other adults. Their competence is not challenged; there is little shaping of any project since one never finishes anything. No self-verification is possible when there's been no cooperation with others, no participation in a common cultural endeavor, nor any novel problem to be met and solved. Then why, say the skeptics, do some women like homemaking?

Women who are happy in housework and the domestic role (and here, for the moment, I am excluding child rearing) usually have taken some domestic task and raised it to a creative art. They cook and entertain beautifully and often, or they design and sew their own clothes, or they redecorate, or garden, or refurnish furniture or some combination of all of these. Many have become proficient in some craft or art as well, which through long habit seems domestic and feminine. Finally, many women happy with homemaking can share in their husband's work to an unusual extent and have the means to enjoy a very creative leisure, as well. Staying at home and not working gives them time to go out. They participate fully in the leisure culture of the community. Moreover, many of these satisfied stay-at-homes who do not "work" are in reality working at a very high level in volunteer work which they "don't count."

It is unfortunate and confusing that "work" has come

[6] Alva Myrdal and Viola Klein, *Women's Two Roles: Home and Work* (London: Routledge & Kegan Paul, 1956), p. 37.

to be identified in our culture with a job. Therefore, when one talks of the innate need to work, many people picture the drab, dreary jobs they have known. Naturally, they protest the idea that *anyone* would need such drudgery. Nor can the criteria of satisfying work among the affluent be measured by a salary. There are many significant and important kinds of work to do that will never be salaried. No one in any corrupt establishment, for instance, will pay someone to lead a reform movement, or to tutor slum children, or picket for peace. The feminist movement itself has been work which did not have the status of being salaried or the prestige of being a professional activity. Work satisfaction is subjective.

The ego is satisfied in work and needs work in which there is cooperation with others in purposeful behavior as well as the satisfaction and self-verification of shaping the environment. In our culture these will most often coincide with going to work for money. The alternate work opportunities described above are rarer. The money for most people is a sign that the work is appreciated by others. Money also lets the worker participate in our money-based culture. Furthermore, even going to a dullish job may provide more novelty and challenge than staying home. The change of location and the presence of other adults will be more stimulating than the isolation of home. Or, in some cases, in a crowded home, going to work is a relief; it is a neutral, less emotionally chaotic way to relate to people and use aggression constructively.

Since there is little structure in American life outside of work, participating in a job may give some welcome structure. Going to work may be the one place most Americans go. Having time off from work defines seasons and the passing of time. Something as minor as having to dress to go to work may aid in a woman's self-verification. The extra challenge of organizing her domestic tasks in a more limited time makes them more interesting. Work provides an outlet for energy and participation in the adult life of the society. Bringing home a salary makes the woman feel a more equal member of the household in a culture which measures power through money-making ability. Friends at work can also enrich the limited social contacts of many people who do not live near their families or childhood friends.

When, in addition to these extrinsic considerations, the work itself is challenging and intrinsically rewarding, then the ego development and exercise of competence makes work a pleasure in every way. While many women who work also enjoy work in the home, work at a job or a profession can be far more satisfying. Basically, the continuing rise in the number of women working can be attributed to the joys of work, extrinsic and intrinsic. Women work because, being human, they want to. Wanting to work in our culture is perfectly understandable. Having developed properly, one will have competence, and a strong ego will want to exercise this competence in the fullest way possible. To be challenged and to interact with the environment and shape it is a sign of maturity. Feminine ego strength is not that different from masculine ego strength. A mature person, male or female, is a good worker and can work and love with ease. It's all right to want to work.

2

What Does a
Good Mother Do?

All right, granting that a mature woman should want to work, does it make a difference if she is a mother? Since femininity is no barrier to maturity and ego strength, strong feminine egos will want to exercise competence and shape the environment. A womanly woman will be a good worker. Moreover, the way this society is set up, this innate urge to act and do with others will usually mean a job or profession. Usually, mature feminine workers will want to "go to work."

But doesn't this all change with the advent of children? Will a mother have this same urge to work? If she does want to work doesn't that prove something is wrong with her as a mother? The traditional assumption has been that working and motherhood are antagonistic kinds of activity. Working has been seen as a rejection of children and the maternal role. The old either/or bind rises again; either you are a good worker or a good mother.

This is a false accusation arising from distortions in our culture. In fact, the very opposite is true. Good workers are good mothers and vice versa. The very qualities which make good workers are those which make good mothers. The good worker is someone with a strong ego who having obtained competence wishes to exercise capacities with others in order to shape the environment toward purposeful goals. The consistency, activity and purposefulness of the worker gives self-verification and self-respect.

These qualities of maturity and strength which make people able to work well, also make them able to love wisely and to mother well. Working is the best preparation for the maturity necessary in motherhood. As one empirical study of mothers and children noted: "In fact, if a woman shows a certain amount of interest and involvement in her work, whatever it is, the prognosis is better for her interest in (and enjoyment of) motherhood. . . . One cannot but wonder whether enjoyment of outside work and motherhood are not both reflections of an underlying "style" of dealing with whatever life situations the individual woman finds herself in." [1] One really need not wonder about this underlying style because it is obviously that of the active coping person, enjoying doing things and cooperating with others. Strong people like to give and do, with and for others; they turn out from themselves to the environment.

The self-acceptance, energy, enthusiasm, and good sense which make good mothers also make good workers capable of good careers. A psychiatrist who has specialized in analyzing women in our culture has this to say on the question: "The dichotomy would seem to be not between motherhood and career, but between women who do

[1] Robert R. Sears, Eleanor Maccoby, and Harry Levin, *Patterns of Childrearing* (Evanston, Ill.: Row, Peterson and Co., 1957), p. 46.

well in both and women who do well in neither." [2] The good worker and good mother are the same in their strength. It is not an either/or proposition in regard to the potential for success in both mothering and working. Another more subtle dimension to this question of good mothering and strong egos has to do with the ego's imaginative ability to control and conceptualize. It is the thesis of other investigators of maternal attitudes[3] that a strong maternal ego implies a mother who has an ability to conceptualize an inner life of her own. A woman sensitive to her own inner life can conceptualize and recognize her child's inner life. By her sensitive response to the child she develops his ego. Her own strong inner sensitivities, controls, and abilities to make decisions and direct activity to goals (the good worker), help her as a mother to expect and build up inner controls and independent inner activity in her child. A strong, active, secure mother with her own goals can be the mother who gives security to her child and activates his goal-directed behavior. A good worker or good mother has the wherewithal to raise good children.

This gets us further into the question of what good mothers do. Having decided that good workers and good mothers have the same potential characteristics does not solve our basic problem. What do mothers do, and can they do it while working? We can be quite sure that a good worker and a good mother will be similar to each other in their ego strength and maturity, indeed, even the

[2] Joseph C. Rheingold, *The Fear of Being a Woman* (New York: Grune & Stratton, 1967), p. 144.

[3] Jane Loevinger and Blanche Sweet, "Construction of a Test of Mother's Attitudes," in John C. Glidewell (ed.), *Parental Attitudes and Child Behavior* (Springfield, Ill.: Charles C Thomas, 1960), pp. 118, 121.

same person, but that does not mean that a woman can be a good mother and good worker *at the same time.* Having the capacity for both does not guarantee that one will be able to do both at the same time. At this crucial point in the discussion, the women's liberation people and the children's liberation people need to do some hard thinking together.

To begin with, what exactly does a mother do? What makes a good mother and how important is she to her child's development? Does her importance depend only upon her physical presence? Many of the new insights developed about personality theory apply to child rearing, just as they do to woman's development. The discovery of the ego and the importance of cognition and competence in human growth also applies to children. The move away from behaviorism and psychoanalytical orthodoxy has also revised the story of what is going on in the earliest years of personality formation. Yet one of the arguments over mothering still has not been solved. Just how important is the mother-child relationship? Is it correct to maximize or minimize the mother's importance in a child's development?

The maxi-mothering advocates are sure that since the mother *is* the child's environment from the womb through infancy, nothing is so important to a child's development as his mother. Mother's love and mother's care are the most important factors in childhood. At the other extreme, the mini-mothering theorists emphasize the fact that the mother is just one factor in the environment. If she is not too hostile, the other people and things in the environment can release the innately developing characteristics and capacities of the child. Later development is as important as early development, and the group and culture can give the child's intelligence and heredity free play.

Naturally the maxi-mothering theorists feel that separation and the breaking of the mother-child bond is the most important obstacle in combining mothering and work. For the mini-mothering theorists, the main problem in the mother's working is the provision of a stimulating enough environment and properly trained child-care workers. These latter experts emphasize the *kind* of care and cognitive stimulation, rather than the bond between mother and child, with its resulting emotional tie. Fathers, other relatives, and an affectionate community of people, in cooperation with the mother can give the child the essential ingredients of a good start. The mother does not need to be a full-time caretaker, or develop an intense and exclusive relationship with the child.

I think both sides in this argument may be true, but true at different stages of the child's life. At the beginning of life, an almost exclusive mothering relationship (assuming a good mother) is best suited to produce a child with highly developed emotions and highly developed cognitive skills. Later, the environment, the group, and the kinds of care become more important than the mother. The famiy and social constellation in which the child moves becomes more important to his development than the exclusive mother-child relationship. Good mothering may remain the same but the child partner in the enterprise needs experiences beyond mother and home.

It is always extremely difficult to pin down what good mothering is and see how it works at different stages of a child's life. This inability to tidily define good mothering arises from the fact that good mothering is a dynamic ever-changing process of accommodation and dialogue. It's all the more confusing because the mother and child are unique and ever-changing as they relate to each other. Their relationship is always in flux.

The mother brings her hereditary equipment, but also her unique experience and imagination to the relationship. Her history of interaction with others has shaped her, especially her relationships with her own parents. As a mother confronts the challenge of pregnancy, birth, and maturation of her child, she must be able to accept herself as mother and her child as a child. The ability to identify with the child and read his signals will very much depend on the kind of mothering she received. Whatever empathy and imagination consist of, they are communicated from mother to child.

Perhaps human beings, in addition to the resources of conceptualization, are helped in the mother-child relationship by unconscious fantasies and images of being mother and being child. Psychoanalytically oriented investigators of parental attitudes, such as Coleman, Kris, and Provence, find that unconscious fantasies are the ferment of parent-child relationships, not just an irrelevant intrusion. "They are part of the equipment of man for parenthood and probably its essence as far as the psychological equipment is concerned."[4]

Surely the use of fantasy, imagination, and empathy is essential in the ability to get out of one's own personal center and project one's self into another's center of consciousness. If a woman can see things from her own mother's point of view, then she has been freed from her, and can more easily function as a mother herself. If she can de-center and imagine being her own child, then she no longer is trapped as the child she once was; she is also freer to be a mother. This ability to live a double emotional life is the ability of the strong flexible ego, free to

[4] Rose W. Coleman, Ernst Kris, and Sally Provence, "The Study of Variations of Early Parental Attitudes," *The Psychoanalytic Study of the Child*, Vol. VIII (New York: International Universities Press, 1953), p. 24.

move from self to others without getting lost along the way. Significantly, in cases of child battering, the parents could not imagine the child as a child, but only as an equal adversary. The most effective therapy for the family was to provide the battering parent with a substitute mother, enlarging the immature parent's sense of security and his imaginative ability to de-center and have empathy with his child.

Since each mother comes uniquely equipped or unequipped for motherhood, the mother's strengths and weaknesses may be stimulated at different times in the child-rearing process. As the baby develops and needs different things from a mother, different dimensions of a mother's multi-dimensional attitude to her child will emerge.[5] Someone who does less well mothering infants may respond better to a toddler or a school-age child (and vice versa). It takes a mother with a very strong, flexible ego, indeed, to be able to be all-giving and adaptable to an infant and then be able to shift to accommodating her child's changing needs for independence and mastery.

At the same time that the child is changing and growing through stages it is increasingly clear that each child is also unique in hereditary endowment. Although some experts insist that maternal response (even in the womb) preconditions any supposed congenital activity type,[6] other theorists insist more reasonably, that physiological inheritance does make a difference. Inherited body types and sensitivities or modes of sensory perception may be crucial in personality formation. Infants are different before you

[5] Here I follow Sylvia Brody's formulation which criticizes Coleman, Kris and Provence for implying a change in maternal attitudes; in Sylvia Brody, *Patterns of Mothering: Maternal Influence During Pregnancy* (New York: International Universities Press, 1956).

[6] Sylvia Brody, *op. cit.*, and *cf.* Rheingold, *op. cit.*, Chapter 15, "The Mother-Fetus Relationship," pp. 635-662.

begin the game; babies come in all sizes, shapes and temperaments.

The baby's unique temperament or biological endowment may make a huge difference in his relationship with the mother. The particular mix of temperaments may affect the complicated dialogue or chain of events which becomes early childhood experience. Sybille Escalona, in her studies of infants and their mothers, declared that "The patterning of life experience *reflects* the developmental process, and at the same time *determines* the course of development." [7] What a particular baby learns or experiences will depend not only on what stimuli he gets from the environment, but also how he with his unique makeup handles the available stimuli.

A very active baby who is highly excitable may be made frantic by too much social or environmental stimulation. A baby who tends to go to pieces with excitement will do more, better, in calm surroundings with less social interaction. Yet a very quiet child may need a good deal of social stimulation to be activated and have any learning experience from interaction with the environment. So too, inner states of fatigue, hunger, and rage may be very differently experienced. Babys' unique styles of interacting with a unique environment of people, places, and things produce very different experiences. A good mother takes account of the uniqueness of her child's temperament and style, as well as her own, and accommodates her mothering to fit the situation.

Unfortunately, this accommodation of good mothering can hardly ever be defined as doing anything specific. Physical needs and medical needs can be described, but

[7] Sybille K. Escalona, "Patterns of Infantile Experience and the Developmental Process," *The Psychoanalytic Study of the Child*, Vol. XVIII, 1963, pp. 197-265.

knowing the appropriate time and method of application is a matter of empathy and judgment. There have been few detailed studies of mothering, but Sylvia Brody, in her study of patterns of mothering, concluded that good mothering consisted of sensitivity to the baby's need, consistency in actions, and frequency of attention. Less adequate mothers might be sensitive but inconsistent or inattentive, or consistent in doing what they thought should be done, without any sensitivity to the baby. Or a mother might ignore or overdo her care consistently. Inner confidence, maturity of character, and good instruction in maternal skills shaped the good mothering of the warm, experienced mothers who could empathize in a mutual relationship with their babies.

Such mothering gives a baby the best of all beginnings. Along with physical care the mother and baby create together a new self-conscious human being who uses language as the mark of his ability to think and relate to others. Apparently, as mothers give continuous care and relieve the discomforts of infancy, they create an all-important attachment and preference for themselves. Repeated experiences of contact-comfort, happy feeding, and familiar sensory signals gradually provide a baby with a focused personal bond to his mother. Pleasure and a particular person become associated in a patterned sequence of experience.

In the very beginning, the baby probably does not know that he is a separate self apart from the world, nor that he is composed of differently functioning systems. He does not know the difference between his insides and the outside world. The patterning, ordering, and focusing of experience and pleasure on one person, the mothering one, aids the baby's grasp of the world and himself. The dialogue which the mother and baby initiate begins to build up his experience of a self. It is not just a question of the mother's unilateral activity, but of her responding appropriately to the initiating activity of the baby.

An individual self probably comes into existence by acting upon, even struggling against, the outside environment. Passive, helpless experiences of the infant need to be transformed into activity. Active, successful communication and mastery strengthen the self. A chain of repeated personal acts which invokes outer responses verifies a continuity of being. The active urge to do and master (call it work) produces the self-verification of activity and communication which strengthens the self from infancy to old age.

In infancy the dialogue is first nonverbal and then gradually it becomes verbal. The baby signals his need and the mother interprets signals and answers his need. The baby's response provokes the mother's further response. A mutually gratifying interaction builds the bond between mother and child. The baby becoming conscious of another in relation to himself, finally becomes conscious of himself as an "I." When he understands that he is accepted, responded to, and can be consistently observed and cared for by another, then he can accept and observe himself as a permanently existing entity.

The theory is that if caretakers, places and need-satisfactions keep shifting unpredictably, a shaky self-identity results. If no person is preferred to another because no one is pleasurably familiar, then this lack of emotional discrimination has ominous results. Perception has been found to be related to the child's emotions. Apparently when a perception arouses strong emotion or affect, then other competing stimuli are blocked. Therefore, the pleasure or joy in his mother's presence helps the baby attend to or discriminate stimuli in less diffuse ways. Strong af-

fective attachment and strong selective attention go together. Consequently, well-loved, attended, attached,
remembered babies develop their capacities for memory
and attention.

Babies who have not had human partners and have
been kept in hygienic and totally impersonal environments have been observed to deteriorate alarmingly. Emotional scars have often been found in children who were
filed away like packages and given no warm, human love
and attention. In the infant's fusion of perception and
feeling, self and experience, subject and object, the constancies of perception and the constancies of loving care
lead the child from self-enclosed autism to objective reality and other people. Love and a human bond lead the
infant and child from viewing people as they gratify to
relating to people who are valued in themselves.

With a familiar, loving person consistently taking care
of his needs, the baby feels safe in a predictable world.
When energy is not being expended simply on "security
operations" [8] the baby has energy to attend and explore
the ever-fascinating world. He initiates what has been
called the child's love affair with the world. Babies learn
through their active exploration and their dialogue with
things, as well as their dialogue with other people. In
developing language, the child's innate capacity to learn
language is dependent upon a partner who engages in a
dialogue with him. The child says something, maybe leaving out verbs or clauses. His human partner expands the
sentence and corrects the usage; the child learns induc-
tively from hearing and conversing. Much of our later
cognitive functioning is dependent on this informal lin-

[8] Harry Stack Sullivan, "Later Mental Disorder," *The Collected
Works of Harry Stack Sullivan*, Vol. I (New York: W. W. Norton,
1953), p. 346.

guistic learning. Middle class children may be ahead of deprived groups, simply because they had mothers or partners who had the time and interest to talk to them.

Good mothering is a process of activating the child through love and attention. The mother can be seen as an enticer into life who fills physical needs and provides beneficial experience. The emotional bond makes the process easy and delightful, mostly a form of play and enjoyment. By consistent, sensitive, attentive care the mother exercises empathy and judgment of what is appropriate at the moment. She must also protect the child from too much stimulation and from being overwhelmed by experience. With security the child will begin to explore and increase in independence. He may come back to the mother for refueling from time to time, but generally the child will gradually grow away from the mother, who must also be able to withdraw at the proper times.

As the child grows up, the same principles of good mothering apply. The mother must still be a provider of experience and protection to the best of her ability. The mutual dialogue continues, only with the child taking more and more of an active part as he matures. Verbal communication supersedes nonverbal dialogue, and in moments of transition and distress, the re-fueling process of childhood may still be needed. In this culture, adolescence is a particularly difficult time for young people and parents. Then the parent can no longer control the environment or the peer group and the dialogue often grows very strained. Raising a child to be an adult who can love and work requires imagination, wisdom, love, and incredible amounts of time and energy.

So we get back to the essence of the problem; can the women who have what it takes to be good mothers and good workers manage both activities at once? The answer will depend on a host of other factors. What is the makeup of the family, how many children are there, and how old? Does the husband support the mother's working? How much outside help does the mother have and of what quality? What kind of work does she do and how demanding is it of her time and energy? How far from home is her work and does she have flexible work schedules which can be adjusted to family life? What support does the society at large give to working mothers? How does everyone concerned view the mother's work, including the mother herself?

Many of these factors to be considered are practical problems, involving social management. More serious is the question of whether maternal accommodation and the all-important mutual dialogue of a loving mother-child bond is harmed by the intervention of other mothering persons. This question has to be looked at from both the mother's point of view and that of the child. In a dialogue and mutual interaction, the subjective perception of each partner is relevant. Just as work satisfaction is subjective and a woman's decision to work depends on her unique makeup and circumstances, so the unique family and social situation determine decisions to have mother substitutes.

Since women as adults can talk, it is easy to assess their feelings about separation from their child. It is more difficult to know the effect of maternal absence or mother substitution upon a child. Lois Murphy, the noted child development expert, has expressed some of the variables from the child's point of view. She says: "Separation, then, is stressful at any time before the child has achieved secure locomotion, speech, self-help, and the capacity to evoke help from others when needed, to orient himself in strange places by his own efforts, to make new relationships with satisfaction and to get and maintain the level of stimulation he needs and protect himself comfortably from excessive demands of the environment." For most American children, these criteria would be met around four or five years old. At this age in this country, in Murphy's judgment, for a normal child, "It is comfortably possible to be separated from the mother for a major part of his waking day."[9]

It is obvious from these quotes that separation from mother is being interpreted as separation from home as well. "Strange places" and "new relationships" require maturity to adjust to. The underlying principle here is that separation is threatening when continuity, love, and communication break down; mother and home are assumed to provide all of these needed relationships. In other words, Lois Murphy is implying that only mother can give the all-important mothering; separation from her means separation from the intimate mothering and the continuous, consistent accommodation necessary for the child to develop properly.

But what if continuity, love, and communication do not break down when mother is absent? When mothering is available from a continuing mother substitute, then the situation is one of concomitant mothering and supplemental mothering, rather than a deficiency of mothering An example of concomitant mothering is the mother substitute who comes into the home. How does this affect the child and the mutual dialogue of good mothering?

Apparently, in the case of a mother substitute who comes into the home, the crucial factor is consistency and the quality of the care. The relationship of the mother to the substitute mother is also important. There should

[9] Lois Murphy, "Some Aspects of the First Relationship," *The International Journal of Psychoanalysis,* Vol. 45, 1964, p. 41.

be no friction nor any great difference in styles or priorities of mothering. A small child should not be confused; nor should a caretaker be excused from disciplining and teaching the child the thousands of things he must learn to be a socialized person. Both goals and methods of mother and mother substitute should be consistent. When the caretaker comes into the home, the child does not have to adjust to a strange place or threatening environment.

Under these conditions of high quality concomitant mothering in the home, the mother's temporary absence does not seem to affect the dialogue or emotional bond. If, that is, the mother is motivated to work for positive reasons and her husband and social circle approves. These other factors in the family and social situation may be much more important than the mother's working and temporary absence. As Eleanor Maccoby, a foremost researcher, concludes from her researches on the subject, "A mother's working is only one of the very many factors bearing upon a child's development. It may even be a minor one. . . ." [10] The older the child, the more true this would be.

Moreover, the higher the status of the work that the mother does, the more she can be seen as a model who controls resources. When she is the employer of the home-helper and controls the child-rearing policy and the environment, then she is still seen as the primary person in the child's life. The mother-child dialogue is not too strained by the addition of a consistent supplemental caretaker. Especially if a mother is absent for only part of the day, or for only several days a week. Often this additional

[10] Eleanor Maccoby, "Effects upon Children of Their Mothers' Outside Employment," *Work in the Lives of Married Women* (New York: Columbia University Press, 1958), p. 151.

adult in the child's life can expand his loving circle of trusted adults. Since the nuclear family has become such a small and isolated unit, some child experts have felt that the presence of another adult may give the developing personality of the child more chance to grow in independence and subtlety.[11] A too-exclusive mother-child dialogue in total isolation from others may also not be the best milieu for mother and child.

When the supplemental caretaker is the child's father then there are added advantages. A father's presence is more advantageous when it is directly experienced rather than indirectly through the father's relationship to the mother and family. Since the liberation of men from the "male tenderness taboo" has also taken place, more fathers are enjoying child care without feeling their masculinity compromised. Today, women can express their need to work, and men can relate to babies in ways unacceptable in the past. Happy the child whose concomitant mothering is provided by his father! But this is still rare.

Most fathers are also at work, so the problem is to find and afford a high quality child-care worker, who will come into the home. Since child care has not been high status work in our society, most women with a developed competence will be doing other kinds of work. Many women who are available for child care have not had any training in maternal skills, nor do they understand the importance of activating the child or engaging in language play. Also, many older women do not have enough flexibility or the happy acceptance of the body's physical functioning that most young mothers would think important.

[11] Leon J. Yarrow, "Separation from Parents During Early Childhood," in Martin L. Hoffman and Lois Wladis Hoffman (eds.), *Review of Child Development Research* (New York: Russell Sage Foundation, 1964), pp. 110-112.

For these reasons, most child experts have been rather conservative in recommending a mother's absence from home before the child is three. A good mother in a good home may be the best beginning for a child. As one psychiatrist sums up the argument, "As a general rule, the child during infancy and babyhood is likely to be more favorably nurtured under the mother's care than under the care of a substitute for her, if for no other reason than the uncertainty of securing an adequate substitute." [12] Many other people concerned with child development also agree.

Two women experts and champions of women's right to work, Viola Klein and Alva Myrdal, agree with those who say "Children First." In order for good mothers and good workers to be *sure* of their child's proper emotional security and proper language development, they recommend staying home until the child is three. As they say, "All through the first few years when the child learns to speak, the presence of one or two stable human companions is of great importance. It therefore seems very desirable that for the first three years of life mothers should devote their time to their children." [13] Many American women who love and enjoy work and also love and enjoy their children have agreed with these child experts. They have not gone back to work, or started to work, with children under three.

However, some women have been able to provide stable high quality concomitant mothers. Either they have an aunt or mother or husband who could care for the

[12] Leo Bartemeier, M.D., "The Children of Working Mothers: A Psychiatrist's View," *Work in the Lives of Married Women,* op. cit., p. 281.

[13] Alva Myrdal and Viola Klein, *Women's Two Roles: Home and Work, op. cit.,* p. 137.

baby in their absence, or they are affluent enough and lucky enough to find and employ a qualified person. When their family and financial situation is good, these women can have their cake and eat it too. They have the pleasures of working and the joys of motherhood. Many of these women find that combining work and motherhood makes them better at both. Work takes up their aggressive energies to shape and achieve, and keeps their children from being unduly worked on. They can relax with their children and relate to them as persons rather than as projects or jobs. Their mutual dialogue with their children is enhanced by their work outside of the domestic sphere.

Many of the women who write of their experiences in this book feel just this way about combining work and mothering. But they also report the difficulties of finding help and support for their combined role. This frustration of many women who would like to work and be good mothers has led many to reappraise our society and see what we are doing wrong. Even worse than the frustration of many mothers who stay home and do a good job is the inadequate mothering that many children of working mothers now suffer. Women who are forced to work are leaving children without adequate care, either through ignorance or desperation.

Because of our own society's failure to solve this problem, both child experts and women's liberation advocates have looked to other countries for a solution. Can the community support women and care for children in a new and creative way? The American movement for day-care and child-care centers has been inspired by other countries' accomplishments. Why can't communal child care also become an accepted part of American life? Could not this solution liberate women and children together?

3

Can Communal
Child Care Liberate
Women and Children?

The most interesting question for those who understand what mothers and children need is whether communal child care can fill both needs at once. Can community care for infants and children during the working day free their mothers to work and exercise their natural desire to cooperatively exercise competence? Can the child-care center give the child the kind of uniquely individual responsive care that a baby gets in a mutual mother-child dialogue? If so, can these communal child-care centers also strengthen the values which most Americans hold to be very important?

Not nearly enough creative thinking has been done on these hard questions. Often women's liberation advocates have flung around references to communal child care and glorified the solutions of other countries without enough study or knowledge of the needs of childen. On the other hand many child-care experts have been too conservative and too committed to our cultural status quo to even consider alternative life styles. For those willing to look and learn from others, perhaps the child-care arrangements in the U.S.S.R. and in the Israeli kibbutzim can help America to come up with more creative solutions to the current crisis. Many new experiments in the current commune movements in the U.S. are also evocative, along with the examples of some small Christian communities. As usual, the Scandinavian countries also lead the way in social experimentation.

The basic problem for most Americans in all communal solutions for child care lies in the power of the collective to determine child-rearing policy and the possible effect of group care upon the child's development.

In the picture of the methods and effect of collective child care which emerges in Urie Bronfenbrenner's sympathetic account of childhood in the U.S.S.R.,[1] this concern for freedom becomes crucial. Their communal child care system is at the service of the state and explicitly shaped to indoctrinate and produce good Soviet citizens. The nurseries, preschools and schools are standardized and directed to this common purpose. Individuality, questioning, and rebellion are not tolerated.

The babies are cared for in the state nurseries with a ratio of one caretaker or "upbringer" for every four babies. The babies are on a "regime" which is a schedule of programmed reenforcement to help them develop motor skills and language skills. Later, in preschool and school, obedience and other values are taught in the same standardized way. Socialist competition is the preferred method. Small groups are urged to compete in work and character building with other groups. The children themselves are given responsibility for enforcing the desired

[1] Urie Bronfenbrenner, *Two Worlds of Childhood: U.S. and U.S.S.R.* (New York: Russell Sage Foundation, 1970).

values and responses; they punish laggards and dissenters with ostracism. Since the rewards of the group depend on the work of all, conformity is enforced.

The worst feature of the collective method in the eyes of most Americans is the encouragement of denunciation of deviant members by their peers. Those children who most conform to the adult's values, i.e., the state's party line, are rewarded with the control of their fellows. Bronfenbrenner also comments on the fact that all the adults in the educational system are women and that girls are usually the most conformist and so put in charge of maintaining collective values. This he attributes to the maternal character of Russian society in which women have outnumbered men for so long. The docility of the Russian child and his dependency on adults and collective security are not challenged by families with the counter-force of strong fathers.

In most cultures in the west, families with strong fathers tend to produce children more given to individuality and achievement, rather than conformity. In Russia, the maternal family and the maternal school and nursery system do not provide any discontinuity or counter-influence to one another. The same values hold in both home and school. The maternal attitude toward the child is restrictive and protective, very loving, but also very demanding of obedience and conformity. Of course, the homogeneity of cultural values has also been bought at the price of great and terrible repression which has removed political opposition or active religious dissent. All in all, the state collective model of communal child care is not a model with much appeal to Americans.

However, there are good aspects of this system which we could well emulate. The whole Russian society is child-centered and involved with the raising of children. Child-care workers and teachers are accorded great respect and supported in their efforts by the parents and society at large. As a rule, many Soviet parents spend more time playing and talking with their children than most American parents, even though the children are in schools and child-care centers for long hours.

Older children and young people consider it a part of growing up to help younger children and become involved in their care. Workers in the community also may "adopt" a class in the local school. The diffuse maternal protectiveness in the culture at large may help ease the children's anxieties over being separated from their mothers. Russian babies and children have a great deal of physical affection and attention lavished upon them. Even the conformist indoctrination is at least at a high level of socialization so that the children do accept idealistic values and feel responsible for themselves and their peers.

And of course, as far as women are concerned, the provision of child care, preceded by maternal medical care for mother and child, does enable mothers to work. Women may not have an idyllic existence in the Soviet Union by any means, but they are encouraged to combine motherhood and working roles. Not, however, for their own fulfillment, but for the greater good of the state. This lack of individual freedom and the necessity of conformity is matched by their lack of control over the policy of the child-care center. If they do not agree that the child should be toilet-trained by 18 months or that the child should be shamed into obedience to the rules by the disapproval of his peers, they can do nothing about it. Americans must try to adopt the best positive features of the system without curtailing certain important freedoms.

In the Israeli kibbutzim, small agricultural settlements committed to a democratic collective life, the children are also the responsibility of the group rather than the parents. Although the kibbutz is a pure democracy de-

voted to equality and parents participate by vote, all decisions on child-rearing policy are made by the group.
The group policy is executed by caretakers, called metapelets, and by teachers. In most kibbutzim the parents are
allowed to have their children visit their rooms for two
hours a day after work, but the children sleep, eat, and
play in the children's houses. In infancy there is one
metapelet for each four babies; after the mother stops
nursing at six months (decreed by group decision), the
metapelet has full charge of the child except for the parents' visiting time.

The child will move from the infants' house to the toddlers' house to the kindergarden to the other older childrens' houses at appointed times, changing metapelets
and getting different teachers. In many kibbutzim the
children sleep alone at night with only a circulating night
watchwoman. These conditions—the changing adults, the
lower ratio of adults to children than in the traditional
family, the fact that the metapelet must also clean the
childrens' houses—ensure that the children make the greatest emotional attachment to their peers who are raised
with them. The peer group gives the greatest support and
from the kibbutz point of view prepares the child to live
the life of the collective comrade. The greatest threat
of disapproval comes from the peer group, since the parents have so little power over the child. The parents
also cannot protect a child from the metapelet or any
part of the group regime.

In theory, having two emotional centers, one the parents' room and the other the childrens' house, produces
benefits. As a noted kibbutz child psychologist claims:
"We believe that there are two emotional centers which
strengthen the infant's ego. Identification with more than
one object mitigates frustrations and conflicts, and com-
pensates for those separations that are due to the necessi-

ties of life. It broadens the images of reality." [2] Other experts and observers concede that "In practice this process has produced as many conflicts as it has resolved. From many points of view, it might well be harder in the long run to adjust to two mothers than to one." [3] Mother and metapelets may have rather different approaches and temperaments; each may feel that the other is not doing a good job, but each is powerless to control the other or to change the situation.

But both metapelets and parents are committed to the kibbutz and by their allegiance to the group apparently provide the child with enough basic security so that his development is not impaired seriously. None of the dreadful consequences predicted by Western psychoanalysts for such a system seem to have come true. One of the best studies of the situation was made by Albert I. Rabin in 1965. The excellence of this study of kibbutz children lies not only in its comprehensiveness and use of systematic procedures, but in the important fact that kibbutz children are compared to other Israeli children who have been raised in villages with a population similar in origin to that of the kibbutz. Western assumptions and prejudices have thus been minimized. A cross section of village and kibbutz infants, ten-year olds, adolescents, and young men were studied and compared by various personality tests appropriate to their ages. [4]

The results seem to show that while the kibbutz babies were behind the family-raised children in a personal-social scale and in speech, [5] the ten-year-olds had more than

[2] Gideon Lewin in Peter B. Neubauer (ed.), *Children in Collectives* (Springfield, Ill.: Charles C Thomas, 1965), p. 72.

[3] Dr. E. J. Anthony, *Ibid.*, p. 127.

[4] A. I. Rabin, *Growing Up in the Kibbutz* (New York: Springer Publishing Company, Inc., 1965), pp. 66-96.

[5] *Ibid.*, pp. 98-103.

caught up, and the adolescents and young men were able to function normally in Israeli society and in the army. The effects on the infants of multiple mothering, especially the changing of metapelets, were marked; but in the long run there was no more serious disturbance in kibbutz children than in our society. The latency child (7 to 12) in the kibbutz however, was considered ahead on all measures. This is attributed to the excellent noncompetitive educational methods and the cooperative support of the children's society at a time when parents are always and everywhere of less importance.

However, a perceptive observer such as Bruno Bettelheim[6] feels that after a sunny childhood, the adolescent in the kibbutz suffers. The kibbutz adolescent will lack the inner richness and complexity that a middle-class child gets from coping with his solitude and his more intense and complicated parent-child relationship. Bettelheim thinks every educational system has its strengths and weaknesses, so while the kibbutz system may sacrifice intellectual heights, and emotional subtlety and richness, it also does not produce homosexuality, drug addiction, abused children, or crime. The support that the child gets from parents, teachers, caretakers, peers, and the whole community equals that of an extended family. These interacting supports compensate for the lack of an intense family relationship.

Since few Americans desire to live in an agricultural commune or can even contemplate setting up children's houses, many of the aspects of kibbutz life are not of interest to us. But what we should learn from these experiments is the resiliency of the developing child's ego. One can get support in many different ways; different dialogues work. Strengths and weaknesses abound in any system,

[6] Bruno Bettelheim, *The Children of the Dream* (New York: The Macmillan Company, 1969), pp. 203-274.

and values can be implemented in different ways. As one of our own child experts has so wisely stated, speaking here only of the American situation, "There is an infinite number of normal variations in patterns of mothering and great diversity in the mode of communication between baby and mother. . . ."[7]

Diversity alone would be a value to most Americans, intent on keeping a pluralistic society filled with free choices. Our society is not homogeneous and the four million or so preschoolers whose mothers are working cannot be quickly moved into a state system as though the U.S. were a kibbutz or a small compact Scandinavian country, whose population is alike in race, creed, and conviction. Nor would most mothers in America relish giving up control over the policies of *their* child's child-care center. Middle-class mothers particularly will never be willing to defer to a system or regime which they cannot shape.

In our country here and now we could better encourage women's liberation and children's liberation by a multi-pronged approach to social change. First, we need a lot of medical aid and education given to mothers and children who need it. Another minimum is some system of family allowance to show that we are seriously on the side of women, children, and the family, like the rest of the developed nations of the world who have this already. Women should also be encouraged to stay home with their children if they choose to, with extended maternity leaves granted as a right by all employers. Since women will probably be having fewer children with the advent of population pressures and improved contraceptive measures, we should realize the importance of this time of life for the child and the precious opportunity and privilege for either mother or child-care worker.

[7] Selma Fraiberg, "The Origins of Human Bonds," *Commentary,* December, 1967, p. 55.

More educational measures for *everyone* in family life and child care should be initiated, perhaps with courses in the schools and community organizations and family apprenticeships or child-care center apprenticeships for young people. If the government supported child-care centers, they could see that many are run by local groups who can control their own policy and the philosophy of child care. If more resource leaders and child-care workers were being educated, this would also bring this work into a higher status; in this event more child-care workers might also work in private homes. With more workers available, several families might band together and hire a high quality caretaker. Small neighborhood centers of several cooperating families could keep the personal unique character of the children's environment, as well as remaining completely flexible to the individual children and mothers.

Mothers themselves can form extended family groupings for sharing child care and create "partner families" to further women's study and part-time work. These cooperative ventures can be between families living close together or in the new extended family communes being pioneered in Sweden and in some parts of the United States. Here the children are cared for and loved by more adults and vice versa. They also have the advantage of more sibling relationships than small families can provide. When more adults and siblings are built into the family circle, separation from the mother does not produce so much anxiety. Also, the different extended families of choice can have their own character and individuality; but the smallness of these groups will not take away the parents' prerogatives or their control over the child's environment.

Another possibility for communal child-care facilities is at places of work. Private businesses and educational

institutions can provide excellent facilities with trained
personnel, so that the family can go to work together.
Mothers and fathers can visit with their children during
the day and vice versa. The opportunity for all adults to
maintain an interest in the next generation and adopt
other children is an important one. The dreadful segrega-
tion of families and work, adults and children has thrown
children back to TV or undirected peer groupings for
their values. Adults and children need to get together to
have a better society. You can't transmit love and values to
people you never come in contact with.

Churches can also rise to the challenge of the present
crisis in our society. Day-care centers run by members
and for members and others can enlarge the world of
children and free more women to work. When the parents
are truly responsible for the values and methods in the
center then their freedom and the continuity between
home and center is helped. Mothers should not be second-
class citizens being instructed and lectured to by alien
experts who take their children away. Caretakers should
strengthen and complement the family. The day-care center should be an extension of home, with "home care."
There have to be enough adults per child, and love,
consistency, sensitivity, with room for solitude and sociability. Also, more men should be encouraged to enter
work with very small children. This is important since
men still have higher status in this country, and many
children need strong male figures to counter-balance a
female-dominated world. Male-led head start groups have
been particularly successful—bypassing many of the dan-
gers of overemphasizing obedience, conformity, neatness
—as in the Russian maternal system. Men in the nurseries
and kindergartens would be extremely salutory. More
husbands could then get involved with child care without
being threatened. Husbands who outgrow patriarchal

attitudes can be a great liberating force for women and children.

The cooperation of men and women in their marriages and in their work would probably be the most Utopian solution of all. If the society at large could break free of the rigid form of the working day and kick the habit of hiring only full-time workers, many families could manage two careers and family life with a minimum of outside help. As several of the women who write of their experiences of combining roles report, the husband's sharing of all tasks on an informal shift system allowed the women to work. Women finally entering the mainstream of American life might be the beginning of a transformation of work in our society into a more meaningful, individualized activity.

The need for men, women, and children to be active and expressive can now be recognized. Giving children more stimulating environments and seeing their development as an active positive growth could be the motivating force and effect of a widespread child-care movement. The children need activity and scope for development; they need more adults and more stimulation, just as their mature and competent mothers do. Everybody needs family life and some work life among cooperating peers. Sometimes this work coincides with jobs and school. Then people are lucky. Sometimes this work will be more informal, artistic or more domestically centered. We need greater flexibility in our work definitions, too. Several of the women who wrote in this book deny that they "work" when working is understood in the old rigid definition to be more akin to mechanical drudgery.

Many of us feel that in this crisis in our culture we may be able to make creative breakthroughs in the way people live in this country. Work can be transformed and expanded, family life can be transformed and expanded, and children can be brought up more humanely. We can use what looks good in other cultures, and discard the aspects of collective life which curtail freedom and individual development. Individuality and pluralism of choices are very precious to us as a people. We need more community, but always with the freedom to choose and change —and with the family as a counter-force. The group is necessary for individual development, for both women and children, but if the group is not to have too much psychic pressure, the individual has to have somewhere to go if he dissents.

In order to make this important point of variability in life style and a pluralism of choices, I tried to ask different kinds of women doing different kinds of work to answer my questionnaire. (*See Appendix.*) I have always thought one of the missing elements in the mass of material about women's employment was the subjective testimony of women themselves.

To me ideological or statistical approaches do not hold the fascination of that particular human ability, the ability to make a verbal report, or "tell it like it is." There's no substitute for the individual's conscious analysis of what she was trying to do, and how she felt about it while she was doing it. You can't even tell whether people are deceiving themselves, unless you know what they think they are doing. Ideals and influences on people, or their own perception of their family background, also help in understanding what goes on in a particular situation.

Thus in my questions, which I either asked personally or sent in a written questionnaire, I concentrated on subjective feelings and evaluations. Though I tried to get women of different ages and backgrounds, I can see after the fact that the middle-class urban women from 30 to 45 is overrepresented. However, this isn't too disastrous since these represent the most influential group of American women today. What these women aspire to do today, most women in America will do tomorow. Mobility, urbanization, the communications media, and education make us all more or less middle-class.

I have a few more doubts about the obviously outstanding women represented here. They might have been exceptions and successes in any culture, at any time. Yet perhaps the fact that they have been professionally successful as married women with children will encourage more women to see new possibilities in their own lives. Besides, the common problems involved in good mothering in modern America can create a bond reaching across lines of class, race, education, religion, and profession. The common desire to be a good mother is expressed by all, but many of these women still take very different approaches to the problem.

It is essential to remember that each woman is unique and faces her unique situation with her own ideas, emotions, and resources. A few women represented in this collection saw few problems in combining children and career; others were burdened with conflicts. Some of these women were so compelled by economic necessity that they could not afford the luxury of worry. Others were so compelled by their psychic need of work, that they too never worried about their decisions. Some of the women felt the pull of both home and work very forcefully.

Obviously the influence of the women's own family and formative culture played a large part in her attitudes. The black women and the women whose mothers were professionals accepted women's work as natural. The Catholic women who were influenced by a whole philosophy defining women's role in marriage had more difficulty making choices. Naturally, attitudes toward family planning were often involved in planning for work, although many of the women expressed an enthusiasm for big families as well as for work outside the home. One also gets impressions from these reports of every variation of domestic life style, from a rather formal, traditional, and organized family life to extremely informal and spontaneous arrangements.

There is only one area of universal agreement; that is the importance of the husband's approval of a woman's work. While some women reported various types of tension with their husbands, all agreed that a woman's work should be a husband-wife decision. All the women thought their husbands had to support their work in principle, although there was every variation in how much practical help husbands were expected to give. Some husbands never lifted a finger to help with house and child care, and some shared fully in all domestic life. Different attitudes to outside help were also reported. Similarly, the children of these working mothers were reported to have a full range of reactions to their mother's work. Every emotion from resentment to pride to nonchalant acceptance is reported. Many times children in the same family were said to react differently.

Perhaps the variability of these reported experiences may help destroy any remaining stereotypes or automatically negative responses to the working wife and mother. Perhaps too, women reading the experiences of other women will be given some insight as they reflect on their lives and make their own decisions. One of women's decisions as a common interest group should also be to band together to get what they and their children need. Even those perfectly satisfied with their own solutions must take responsibility for the well-being of other women and children. Having thought the problem through carefully, let us act. In the meantime a few of the women most involved can here speak for themselves.

4

MARGARET O'BRIEN STEINFELS

My Working Mother Problem and Theirs, or Who Put the Overalls in Mrs. Murphy's Chowder?

Margaret O'Brien Steinfels is in her mid twenties. She is a married graduate student with one three-year-old girl. She has held a variety of jobs and regularly writes free-lance reviews and articles. Her questioning of the American work ethic is typical of a great number of younger people. Women's traditional ambivalence toward professional careers has become part of a general cultural phenomenon.

Whatever I might say about working mothers suffers from an unnerving credibility gap. Not unlike our politicians I talk out of both sides of my mouth on the question. At parties, I try to be two steps to the left of the most radical; in my kitchen only two steps behind my daughter. After two scotches and a handful of peanuts I am always willing to raise the ante to communal or husband child rearing. In my kitchen, more or less sober, I see myself for what I am: a radical practitioner of delaying tactics: still going to school, still pleading ignorance, still encouraging my husband to wrap the garbage in the help-wanted section.

The only explanation I can give for this apparent hypocrisy is that the public discussion isn't carried on in terms into which I can inject my personal experience. The terms of that discussion, at least in the circles where I agonize, have been laid down by books like *The Second Sex, The Feminine Mystique,* and their derivatives. The harried mothers, the victimized wives, and the repressed women who rallied under those flags have, I am told, found their freedom. My problem is certainly no more profound than theirs; it is simply different. Their's fell on the woman-wife-mother half of the proposition; mine falls on the working half.

As I duck under that credibility gap let me shift the cigar to the other side of my mouth and blow a little smoke in the opposite direction.

I am 27 years old, have been married five years, and am the mother of a three-year-old daughter. My husband and I started our marriage with some romantic notions about equality and everyone doing his thing that remain intact. From a statistical point of view he has fared better than I, but then, he has been more certain about what he wanted to do and has industriously gone about doing it. He is a writer and an editor, finishing his work on a Ph.D. In contrast, I have been certain about nothing and my efforts have been correspondingly diffused.

We were married a few months after college graduation. By that time I had held a variety of jobs, enough to convince me that money wasn't the stimulus I needed to keep working. On the other hand, a liberal arts degree in history didn't fit me for much of anything but going to graduate school, and my precise interest at the time,

ancient history, didn't augur well for my ever doing anything *but* going to school. So, in a manner of speaking,
marriage offered me a respite from decision.

The economics of all this equality were supported by my
husband's various and sundry fellowships. They don't
qualify anyone for life in middle-class America, which is
usually all right with me, but they certainly give one
enough to live on if necessities are defined by the amount
of money on hand and not vice versa. This decision to live
on the money supplied us meant that I was free to follow
my whims as far as occupations were concerned. And five
years ago, after sixteen years of school, all I wanted to do
was sit down and read a book, all the way through.

The limitations of solitary book reading became apparent quickly enough—after about two weeks. Consequently, I jumped at the chance to help edit a small, non-
paying magazine that reflected some of my interests in
student problems and allowed me to do a great deal of
writing.

At about the same time, in what I have always suspected
was an attempt to wean me away from my first attempts
at gourmet cooking, my husband bought me a copy of
The Feminine Mystique. It crushed me with the thought
that I might be suffering from "the problem without a
name." Life was too serious a business to be spent grating
Parmesan cheese and beating up a chocolate mousse—alas.
In fact, life was so serious that one's self-identity could
only be gained and maintained under categories of professional titles, monthly paychecks and participation in
the Gross National Product.

More or less at this point of rising identity crisis the
small magazine passed out of my existence and I lost
my only good excuse for not really working. Under the
dictatorship of the feminists, of course, laziness won't do.
So with the hope of wedding a personal interest with some

sort of future job, I decided that my perennial sidelines, painting, pasting, drawing, and cutting, could be whipped up into a career. What's more, I could probably do it while keeping my eye on a pot of home-made noodles and, by the way, would also avoid supervision and a nine-to-five schedule.

As I began art school I also found a part-time job working for a book illustrator, who thankfully needed not my talent so much as my ability to draw a straight line with a ruler and paste *neatly*. This job and art school were marvelous; it was working home alone that ruined me. Such an asocial, nonverbal occupation was as bad as solitary book reading and, alas, was not what I wanted either.

This waning interest in being an artist corresponded with the growing presence of my daughter, Gabrielle. My self-image reeled under another blow. Of course, I still had the same possibilities and potentialities. The notion of working mother wasn't unknown to me—my mother had worked and raised a family as had my grandmother. It was the mother image pure and simple. Who in this day and age wants to be a mother and will admit it—nag, martyr, sapper of her husband's virility and her children's independence?

And even in my weakened-image condition, if these larger problems didn't come marching in, I still worried about future nights spent walking the floor, of days brimming with dirty diapers, of taking my appointed place in the park, and, that in the end, nothing more true than "She was a good mother" would appear on my gravestone. This sense of fatefulness beat strong enough in the weeks before Gabrielle was born to send me into total panic. I signed up for a French course, a history of film course, and agreed to write movie reviews for another small magazine.

Gabrielle was born August 20th; I returned to school September 20th. My little fortress of precautions proved useful, but weren't, after all, so necessary. Things can't go too badly when you're expecting the Cheshire Cat and who should turn up but Alice herself.

Gabrielle was the perfect baby and I was a happy mother. She slept through the night from the beginning, had, like most babies, only one dirty diaper a day, and the other mothers in the park were as busy as I, reading *Civilizations and Its Discontents*. Gabrielle's first year allayed my anxieties about motherhood, forced me to be more disciplined about my work, and brought out Peter's previously unsuspected mother instinct. Since one or the other of us was usually at home, Gabrielle acquired more than her share of Erik Erikson's famous commodity—basic trust. (We keep the excess in a piggy bank.) Brunhilde, her psyche, whom she keeps in her apron pocket, has stood up in the two years since under a variety of baby-sitters, two trans-Atlantic voyages, and a daily lack of schedule.

And if a year of being taken care of by her parents was good for Gabrielle, it was also very good for her parents. Our somewhat cerebral existence took on a new, earthy tone and even if our dedication to the *nouvelle vague* was curtailed, she more than substituted for everyone but Fellini.

Because social pressures are off for "a mother in every pot," it is getting terribly difficult to use children as an excuse for not working. As Gabrielle's first birthday approached I was still shamelessly using her for my wanton ways. It was time for a reassessment.

With the pre-negotiation agreement that *this time* our decision would be irrevocable, poor Peter and my poor self-image sat down to Episode 27 of "What Should I Do with My Life?" After the usual exorcisms and book burning (our fifth of *The Feminine Mystique*) and three months of talks, we issued a statement to Gabrielle saying:

As a one-year-old, it's time you grew up and mama settled down. Enough sitting around playing with you, reading three magazines, two newspapers, and a book every day. Enough lasagna, lemon meringue pie, and scrambled eggs; from now on its TV dinners, popsicles, and raisin bran. Enough of these crazy conversations until two and three in the morning; from now on, early to bed, early to rise. Irrevocable decision: Mama begins work on M.A. in American history, finishes in a year and a half, keeps writing, takes a teaching job part-time in two years while working on Ph.D.

Gabrielle smiled knowingly, applauded the resoluteness of our decision and we began our search for the worthy sitter.

Since we live in New York City this wasn't very difficult. Even part-time sitters, which my irregular schedule and our vague economic situation warranted, weren't hard to find. The first place we turned was the student employment agency of the large university in our neighborhood which regularly supplied us with an adequate if generally unenthusiastic stream of women college students. My estimates of their worthiness went down as their prices went up and I then found a high school girl who was able to take Gabrielle to the park for two or three hours every day. A friend was able to babysit several afternoons a week during the few months before her own first child was born. And for one glorious three weeks, another friend lent us her housekeeper. For the first time in our familial history we had a clean baby and a clean house too.

But the home of the vintage sitter is France. Since Gabrielle was born, my husband's studies have brought us here twice. Two summers ago she was spoiled but loved by a succession of French school girls. This year we are

living in Paris, where she is watched every morning by
what may be, if industrial society takes root in France,
the last of the world's great nannies. Needless to say, there
are no words in the English language worthy of describ-
ing her.

Despite the ease with which we solved our baby-sitting
problems, I am, after two years, rather behind on my irrevocable decision, although my *quiche lorraine* gets
lighter and lighter. Having completed only half the requirements for my master's degree I probably will not
finish it for another year. And while my teaching plans
hang in abeyance, my intention of working on a Ph.D.
had faded into an uncertain future.

With all of my best intentions, clearly I am nobody's
ideal worker, mother or no, and I probably never will
be. What is less clear, even to me, is why this should be
so. My mother successfully combined the two; my education has been adequate for finding a job; my husband
has encouraged me to continue with school and to work
when I wished; general social pressures have pushed me
toward finding a job rather than staying at home.

Psychiatric counseling is the order of the day for any
27-year-old man who might have acted in the same way.
In contrast, I frequently receive clucking notes of sym-
pathy for my supposedly valient, but half-successful efforts. It is, after all, society's lack of concern for women
that makes it difficult for me to finish my education
quickly, to find reasonably-priced full-time, competent
child care, to compete on the job market with men who
are considered the more reliable workers. All these road
blocks are real enough, but they are not in themselves the
real cause of my dilatory ways.

It is more a problem of will. I find it increasingly difficult to decide that working from nine to five, five days

a week, on civilization building, is all that interesting. At the heart of my reluctance is a deep suspicion of what passes for achievement in American society and, to be concrete, what passes for self-fulfillment in the world of work.

Even though we have, as so many economists tell us, passed from an era of scarcity ruled over by a Calvinist work ethic into a paradise of abundance, work maintains its moral primacy and remains a crucial factor in the way we identify people, including ourselves. Or rather, not so much *work*, but "jobs."

Black men are told that their wives, their families, and society would respect them if they found a job. Black women are told that their families would have more moral fiber if they went to work and got off the relief roles. White women are told that their husbands would respect them and their children love them if they went to work. And the white male drop-outs—the hippies, the young revolutionaries, the perennial students, the acid heads—are being held up as terrifying examples of cultural anarchism.

To put things on the simplest level, I do not like the 40-hour week, the regimentation, the competitiveness, the aggressiveness, the search for prestige which powers our economic activity—including that of intellectuals and professionals. We need vast numbers of doctors—why not women? But women doctors must practice their profession in that combination of petit bourgeois virtue and big business which defines medicine in the United States today. The healing function, a traditional "womanly" activity in our mythology, must be transformed into a commodity before it can be linked to science and education. We need vast numbers of good teachers—why not women? But women teachers must practice their professions within the frequently asylum-like structures of primary and secondary school systems, or within the mixture of medieval hierarchy and modern bureaucracy that defines our universities. Those who must can learn to live with these conditions. But please pardon my skepticism when I hear the entry of women into this world of work labeled "liberation."

The schizophrenic attitudes I have toward working mothers are reflective, then, of the divisive tendencies that I think are at work in our society and our economy. With all due allowance for the charms of alcohol, what may inspire my fervent support of working mothers at parties is the consensus one finds in such gatherings that the new possibilities open to women because of birth control, education, and technological households have profoundly changed her role—changes which should result not only in new forms of family life, but also in new forms of work. Thus far, however, the role of the new woman has been defined in terms of the Old Economy, rather than in the possibilities of experiment which seem to me to be one of the great promises of the abundant economy. Since I don't much care for the Old Economy, I dally reluctantly in school and in my kitchen.

I'd be happy to find a solution to my dilemma. I don't really plan to pass the next fifty years over a pot of chocolate pudding, reflecting on the deeper symbolism of "Who Put the Overalls in Mrs. Murphy's Chowder." I pursue my academic aims despite my many moments of skepticism, hoping to be able to do my bit in the great jigsaw puzzle. Perhaps under the strain of the working father problem, my husband will send me out to take my turn in the Old Economy. Yet the doubt remains. To borrow James Baldwin's question about another historic change, "Why integrate into a house on fire?"

5

SUSAN STUART, M.D.

More Than One Doctor in the House

Dr. Susan Stuart is the pseudonym of a physician who with her husband is an instructor at a University School of Medicine. She and her husband married while in medical school and have pursued their careers together. Coming from a family of physicians, including her mother, Dr. Stuart considers a career normal. Now in her early thirties, with two small daughters, a cooperative husband and adequate help, she finds little conflict in combining career and family.

Paper-back novels about women doctors usually have a strikingly lovely girl on the cover, and some sort of legend about "Should she continue serving humanity . . . or should she marry the man she loves?" Love nearly always triumphs, except when the man involved turns out to be a perfect cad and she returns to healing humanity to heal herself. Real-life women doctors don't usually have those problems. For one thing, they tend not to be strikingly lovely; for another, there need be no choice between a medical career and a happy marriage. Hard work, an understanding husband, and a resilient sense of humor are all essential, but the net combination of marriage and a challenging career is worth the effort. My experiences may not be typical of other women doctors, but I am not writing a sociologic study of the doctor-mother; I can only give my own history.

I am a pathologist in my early thirties. My husband, Paul, is a psychiatrist. We met and married in medical school, and completed our internships together. Specialty training has taken us into diverging paths, but, except during Paul's stint in the armed forces, we have always worked at the same hospital. Our two daughters, aged six and four-and-a-half, were born during my years of pathology training. At present, both Paul and I teach and practice our specialties at a medical school, and I direct one of the hospital laboratories.

From the birth of our first child, I have had a maid five-and-a-half days a week. We did not consider taking the children to a nursery or leaving them with a neighbor. Maids are difficult to find and expensive, but, to my mind, fully worth the trouble and expense whenever possible. I have been fortunate in finding reliable, pleasant women who share my basic approach to child rearing. The children remain in their own home, a secure and familiar territory which provides continuity even if the maid must change. They feel they are welcoming a friend who comes to them; they don't feel they are packed away for my convenience. Although they have seen their mother leave home six days a week from their earliest infancy, they have equally seen a beloved friend come to take care of them. Far from feeling abandoned, they are surrounded by those who love them.

I, too, value the security that minor childhood illnesses can be treated at home without my leaving work when a child cannot attend nursery school. Severe illness, of course, would require my presence, but we have, mercifully, been spared any. An absolute requirement for a working mother is healthy children. If a child is chronically ill or suffers repeated bouts of severe illness, the mother cannot devote the necessary time or energy to a career. If the woman herself suffers poor health, she might continue her career if she is stoic enough, but she simply can't jeopardize her children's health.

Having a maid also gives me time for those I love. Before we started our family, my husband and I cleaned house together in our free time. When I bought clothes, they had to be drip-dry or I wouldn't get them, no matter how becoming they were. We made complicated plans for delivery of large items or for receiving repair men. In short, most energy left over from medical training went into the mechanics of living. As our family and careers have grown, the mechanics of living have become increasingly complex, while time available has diminished with increasing domestic and professional responsibility. If I had to clean the house, run the laundry, do the ironing, and polish the silver after a full day at work, I would certainly shout at the children and ignore my husband out of sheer fatigue. Since my husband has always shared the houshold burdens, he, too, found the arrival of the maid a godsend.

A maid doesn't do everything. I do my own marketing, shopping, and cooking. A maid can't go to the hairdresser for me, or attend the children's school programs in my place. Many of these tasks can be done in the evening, since stores and shops now recognize the needs of working women and remain open for long hours. But most are more easily and pleasantly done during the day, and children's activities must be done during the day or not at all. The career I have chosen permits me to do all these things, but at a price.

The price is responsibility. As a general rule, the more responsibility a job demands, the more personal freedom it offers. If I had to answer a telephone or sell at a counter eight hours a day, free time during the day would consist only of a limited lunch break, but evenings and weekends would be my own. As a physician running a laboratory, I have relatively few fixed obligations. Lectures and teaching sessions occur at specific times, but I can rearrange most other work according to my own schedule. The obligations do not, however, cease at 5 in the evening. I may take several hours off during the day, but the phone may ring at any hour of the night or weekend. Usually I need not return to the hospital, but a long session of hair-tearing and telephone calls is likely to follow.

I have a salaried position in a large medical center. The private office practice of medicine would offer far less flexibility, and for this reason relatively few women doctors with young children are in private practice. In salaried or group practice, someone else can take charge for a few hours, and coverage is available for vacations or unexpected crises. Often such an arrangement means a lower income or diminished chance for professional prominence, but the rewards in home and family are worth this sacrifice.

Our daughters may not, objectively, be as beautiful as we consider them, but even teachers, babysitters, and neighborhood mothers agree that they are unusually happy, healthy, and well-behaved children. They would almost certainly be less happy and probably less well-behaved if I were home with them all day. I am not a notably patient individual, and prolonged exposure to their voices, noise, needs, and demands begins to wear me down. Teaching pathology and running a laboratory wear me down too, but fortunately the two set of problems are completely different. I am delighted to leave the house in the morning, and delighted to return in the evening. The hours from 7 to 8:30 A.M. and from 5:00 to 8 P.M. are not, perhaps, the best hours for peaceful home scenes, and there is certainly stress and strain some days. For the most part, though, I can give the children my full love and attention while I am home, and on Saturday afternoon and Sunday we have the whole day together for more leisurely activities.

Since the children are not accustomed to my continual presence, they are not notably alarmed by occasional absences. They know that their mother, like their father, goes away and then comes back. As a result, they have tolerated our occasional overnight absences with good grace, even though the babysitter has never been the regular maid. As they have grown older, Paul and I have been able to take several very pleasant trips alone together.

Ours is not a child-centered household. Both Paul and I had parents who expected that children would have their own interests and enthusiasms, and it was clear that the adults' lives included, but did not revolve around, the children. We both feel that children are an extension and enrichment, but not the sole embodiment, of our love for each other. We spend a great deal of time away from our children, but the time we devote to them is fully theirs. On weekdays, this includes a fairly relaxed family breakfast and the time between the children's dinner and their bedtimes. On the evenings that Paul is home, he and I eat together while the children play upstairs. They are invited to say the blessing with us and sample what we are eating, but they do not remain for the whole meal. In this way, we have a more varied and adventurous menu than we could have if we all shared the table, and the children learn that dinner is a time for the relaxed enjoyment of good food and conversation. Although there are many nights when my husband gets home after the children are asleep, they seem to suffer no lack of paternal attention, and both are—quite heathily—little Daddy's girls.

Both girls will probably grow up to have careers, and the chances are that at least one will follow me and my mother into medicine. Not only are Paul and I physicians, but my father, mother, grandmother, and uncle are all doctors, as is my husband's brother. As I was growing up, I felt no family pressure directing me specifically into medicine, but there was a definite expectation that I would have a career of some sort. I could have chosen social work, teaching, newspaper work, or retailing (all of which I considered before my third year in college) without any family problems, but the decision to take a stop-gap job until early matrimonial retirement would have met with raised eyebrows. My mother clearly considered motherhood a satisfying part of her life, but not the only reason for her existence. Our home was a place where four interesting people lived together, sharing a number of common interests, but each pursuing individual goals. My brother's goal was not medicine; his field is corporate finance. My mother's attitude toward domestic pursuits was one of amused tolerance. As long as a maid kept the house reasonably clean, she would do the marketing and the cooking, but without investing undue time in either. A daughter growing up in this atmosphere would probably take one or the other of two opposite approaches to life. Either she would reject the independent role to become a devoted nest-builder, or she would adopt a similar attitude of individual attainment.

Obviously, I share my mother's basic approach to life, but I prefer to invest a little more time in domestic amenities. I am delighted that someone else does my cleaning and laundry, but I enjoy cooking, sewing, and entertaining, and I spend far more time in the kitchen than my mother considers rational. In fact, my major leisure interest besides reading is cooking. This interest is shared by my husband, and together we collect cookbooks and enjoy trying new recipes, exploring foreign food stores, and savoring first-class restaurants when we visit large cities.

My husband and I are in full agreement about careers for married women. Since we met and married in medical school, it was apparent from the start that I would be a working wife. In moments of professional discouragement, I sometimes mention abandoning medicine to become a housewife, but Paul turns a deliberately deaf ear. He realizes, probably more clearly than I do, that my training, education, and personality before marriage were directed toward individual achievement, and I could never be happy if keeping house and raising children were my only outlets.

Whenever the wife works outside the home, the marriage must make certain adjustments, but the motive for the wife's working inevitably affects a marriage. The woman who works because her income keeps the family out of financial straits must surely feel differently toward the rewards and trials of employment than the woman who chooses a lifelong career, and so will her husband.

Unless the husband is fully in favor of his wife's career, the marriage or the career, or both, will surely fail. The more challenging, time-consuming, and absorbing her profession, the more whole-hearted his cooperation must be. He must, after all, put up with a certain number of delayed meals and emergency stints as babysitter, and a lifetime of shirts that are not laundered lovingly by his wife. On the other hand, the wife had better decide quite early where her basic responsibilities lie. My own conviction is that husband, children, and home come first, and medicine must accept the time and energy that remain. I am a pathologist because pathology is an exciting specialty, and also because it can be combined with a relatively normal home life. I know that, as a wife and mother, I am unlikely to attain either the money or the professional renown possible if my entire energies went into medicine.

My career has also required some sacrifice on Paul's part. Certain types of medical training and practice require almost total devotion. If Paul chose to adopt such an approach, I would have to give up some or all of my career, since the children should have at least one parent they see regularly. I doubt that Paul consciously chose to abet my career by avoiding such a demanding practice. If he had wanted that kind of life, he would have chosen a different kind of wife. However, if we move from our present positions or decide to leave academic practice, our choice will rest upon his advancement, rather than mine.

The double demands of career and home sometimes become taxing. Naturally, both men and women in a given profession will have interests outside their work. The difference is that the man's hobby or avocation is optional; its demands can be postponed or adjusted. The working mother has no choice; she has to get the children fed, bathed, and in bed whether she wants to or not. This makes for a very full life. I am frequently tired, sometimes discouraged, and occasionally mad at the whole world, but I am never bored. By judicious budgeting of time and energy, I probably accomplish as much sewing, fancy cooking, current reading, and entertaining as most of our friends. Sometimes I envy the sociability of volunteer work, daytime bridge, morning coffee, and other pursuits of the suburban wife, but if there is a particularly enticing luncheon or fashion show, I can usually manage to go. I do not, however, have many women friends. Most of our social life is as a couple, largely with my husband's associates. I am not a particularly social person. If I didn't work, chances are that I wouldn't have many invitations to coffee or bridge, and rather than do volunteer work on a large scale, I prefer a career.

Both Paul and I believe my career improves, rather than encumbers, our marriage. Because I have an identity other than "Paul's wife," I need not cling to him for self-importance, community status, or contact with the outside world. Since we are both physicians, we can exchange experiences and ideas without preliminary explanations. More important than our common training is the shared understanding that each of us is a complex, creative individual, and our mariage is a deep, growing union from which we each draw strength.

6

BETTY MAYS

Part-time Work
Solves My Problems

*Betty Mays is in her mid-thirties, black, and the
mother of two small boys. She has worked in an office
since her children were born, but for only six hours a
day for six months of the year. This schedule makes it
easy for her to combine work and family. She speaks of
her own work satisfactions and the difficulties many of
her friends have had trying to combine roles in a large
city.*

Q.[1] Could you give me a general idea of why you work?
A. Well, I suppose my reasons are pretty much the
same as most working mothers. I work for the simple
reason I'm more or less cooped up in the house all year
long and want to release some of the tension I think

[1] This account of the experience of combining work and child
rearing was written from a personal interview. Both the interviews
and the essays in this book derived from the questionnaire which
appears in the Appendix.

builds up. I prefer going to work. I have been working now since I had my first baby and I find that working half the year and staying home the other half relaxes me quite a bit. I'm more or less able to cope with the problems at home better than if I was home all day.

Q. So you don't need to do it for the money? It's really for your own peace of mind?

A. Yes. I don't have to work because my husband's income is quite sufficient to support me and the children, but I find that I just want to work; it gives me a certain amount of independence too, I suppose. I really enjoy working, and the work that I do is so interesting I find myself looking forward to it each year.

Q. Did you have a life plan at the beginning of your marriage that included work in addition to child rearing or did it just sort of happen?

A. To be perfectly truthful with you—I didn't really give it much thought. I knew that eventually we were hoping we would have children, but I started working first. I became very interested in it and after the first child I did decide to continue working.

Q. Did you or do you expect to plan your family size with work or further education in mind?

A. Well, I hoped that we had already planned the family size. We wanted two children and we have them so if it is at all possible we'd like to stop there. My working will help with the education plans for the children. I have already started an educational fund of my own for the children aside from what my husband and I have already put aside for them. I feel that my working will more or less help us to achieve the goal that we are working for as far as education is concerned.

Q. Did you make your decision on family size mainly for the sake of your children or as part of your decision to keep working because you enjoy it?

A. We made the decision about the number of children we would have for this reason: We thought that two would be enough and we thought that we could give them a better education than if we'd had more. Our decision was based more on our hopes and plans for our children than on my enjoyment of work.

Q. How old are your children?

A. I have two sons, John, Jr. who is seven and Kerry who is three and a half.

Q. What different problems with your children have you experienced so far as your work is concerned? Was it easier when they were younger or has it gotten more difficult as they've grown older?

A. Well, I worked up until I was in my fifth month of pregnancy with the first one and I stayed home with him until he was a year old. I then went back to work and I worked until he was three; then I became pregnant with my second son. I worked up until six months of pregnancy also with him. I find it's much easier as they get older, because I don't have to be quite as concerned about their welfare as I would have when they were smaller. When they're infants you have to worry about the formula and the diapering and so forth, but by now they are able to go out in the park and play without having to be worried about all the time. And it's getting better.

Q. How have your children responded to your work? Have they been happy with it or do they sometimes cry when you leave in the morning, or do they wish you would stop working?

A. When I first started working with John, Jr. I had problems for a while but not very long because I had a babysitter that he liked very much. After a while he got used to my going to work so I didn't have too much trouble with him. The same thing happened again with Kerry until he got used to the idea that I was going to work. He cried a little in the morning but once I had gone he completely forgot about it. And during the afternoons and the weekends we spend so much time together anyway, I don't think that it really bothers them much.

Q. What exactly is your work schedule?

A. I usually work from October through March and I work from 9:30 A.M. until 3:30 P.M. which isn't very bad because I'm not away from them all day. And John, Jr. is in school now from 8:30 until 3:00, so he's only home about 30 to 45 minutes before I get home. And with Kerry, well, he's not in school now but I'm hoping that he'll be able to start preschool soon. So, I'll only be away from him two or three hours or maybe four hours during the day. But the person I leave him with has children too and there's a small child who is home all day so he more or less has company and maybe more companionship than he would have if he was home with me alone.

Q. You work only during the day, then, when they're at school or somebody's taking care of them and then you stop during the late spring and summer?

A. That's it. That was one of my "musts." My husband and I came to an agreement. He doesn't really want me to work but I more or less insist on it, as I said before, to release some of this tension that I build up all year. And he said that if I wanted to work I could only work five or six months out of the year so that I could be home with the children in the spring and in the summer. The months that I am working are the winter months when they must be in anyway and John is in school and Kerry's with a babysitter. During the spring and summer, when they can go out and play in the park, I prefer being home with them.

Q. What aspects of this whole arrangement or what aspects of your own childhood have given you the greatest concern or worry in pursuing your work?

A. I was reared by my grandmother and she never went to work. So as far as my own working conditions are concerned, there is no relation whatsoever between my childhood and my children's because my grandmother was always there. My mother was away. And as far as any relation between the two I don't see any.

Q. If you were raised with your grandmother always there, have you sometimes worried that you're not there some of the day?

A. Well, sometimes I do think about that too. When the babysitter first started I would worry as to whether she was watching him properly or whether he was in any kind of danger. Not that I thought he was, because the babysitters that I've had so far have been very reliable. I think it's just a natural mother's instinct to worry sometimes about the children.

Q. Did this worry ever have a little bit of guilt in it, maybe wondering whether you were doing the right thing?

A. Yes, it has. There have been one or two occasions when there was a minor accident where he fell and must have slipped; and I thought to myself, "What if I had been home, maybe this wouldn't have happened?" But I had to think twice about that, because I remember when Junie was small the same thing happened while I was at home. So this worrying is just something that comes naturally, I think.

Q. What experiences have you had with mother substitutes or babysitters so far as small children are concerned? If your children have spent a lot of time in the care of others while you work, have you worried about the kind of influence these people would have on your children?

A. Well, no. Because I've never had to stay away from them for a long period of time. I mean the hours that

I am away at work are the longest that I'm away from them, and I don't think that it's quite long enough to give the sitter, you know, a chance to influence them. Also, the people that have taken care of them for me have been people who are friends of mine and are more or less on the same level, except for the working. We more or less have the same ideas about raising children.

Q. Were you raised with the expectation that a woman would combine work and child rearing?

A. Well, I'll answer this way. Even as a child, I was taught to believe that a woman should have a certain amount of independence, and in order to achieve things that you want it might be possible that you would have to go to work to help your husband, but it wasn't compulsory that you do.

Q. Do you have any conflict over your lack of leisure compared to women who do not work?

A. No, because I find being at home all day very boring. Most housewives if they have small children are up around 7:30 or 8 o'clock in the morning, if not earlier, and by mid-morning the housework is done. Therefore, you have the rest of the morning and all afternoon for leisurely doing nothing. I find it very boring being at home and I don't envy them at all.

Q. How do you think our society could be changed or improved to make it easier for women to combine work and mothering?

A. Well, I think they have already started babysitting for mothers who want to work. And I think that's about the best idea that has come about so far. I only recently read that there was a new institution, a place downtown where you could go for help if you wanted to go to work and wanted someone to take care of your children. There are certain women available who didn't have children or who had teenage or grown-up children who would be able to come in and sit for you during the day if you wanted to go to work. That is the best thing that's happened yet for working mothers.

Q. Do you think it would be a good thing if the government, either state or federal, started setting up and organizing child-care centers?

A. Yes, I do think it would be an excellent idea for the simple reason there are a lot of mothers who feel as I do but they're not able to get jobs that pay enough so they can afford a babysitter and still come home with extra money too. If this sort of institution or whatever you might call it was set up, then I'm sure it would allow a lot of mothers who want to go to work to do so without having to worry about whether or not they would be making enough to really compensate them for work after paying somebody to keep the children.

Q. And of course it would help those who actually had to work and needed the money.

A. Yes, it would be a great help to them, sure.

Q. What kind of work do you do? Do you think that your particular line of work makes it easier or harder to combine family life and work?

A. The type of work that I do I find makes things much easier for me all the way around. I work in a subscription department of a magazine and I've been here for ten years with the exception of the times I took off for having my two children. I find the work here is very interesting, it is the type of job that I prefer more than anything else. I enjoy being here so much that I think the idea of spending a few hours here makes me even more relaxed when I get home with the children than I would be if I was home with them all day.

Q. Is the work secretarial with typing, and clerical filing?

A. It is a combination of all that, secretarial, clerical,

telephone relief. Everything that usually goes on in offices. It is the combination of all those which makes it more interesting.

Q. You think this kind of work is maybe easier to combine with a family life than other kinds?

A. I should think so, because I feel that after five or six hours a day here doing this type of work I am not as tired as I would be if I had been on my feet all day.

Q. If you didn't work here do you think that this is the kind of work you could get easily elsewhere? Part-time.

A. Well, I'm not sure whether I would be able to find this particular type of work part-time. And to be perfectly frank with you, if I didn't work here doing this type of work I don't know whether I would be a working mother. Only maybe if I was doing part-time work like answering a telephone or something that wouldn't take all my energy so I would have time for the children. I feel that 9:30 to 3:30 are ideal hours for me. Doing this type of work gives me plenty of time to get home before evening is over and to be with the children.

Q. From your own experience, how would you suggest that young women plan to combine family and work?

A. I feel like this—first of all the husband and wife have to sit down and talk it over. If he feels that it's all right if she works, I suggest that she try to find somebody who is suitable to help her. Somebody that she can really rely on, not just anybody. It has to be somebody that you either know or has been recommended to you by somebody else. Because unless you have someone you can really depend on with your children, you can't work in peace and that's the important thing. So I feel that if there is a young woman who wants to go to work and it's with the agreement of her husband I don't see why she shouldn't.

Q. What mistakes if any do you feel you made in trying to combine family and work? Has your experience taught you things you wish you had known earlier?

A. Offhand I can't think of any, because as I've said before, this is something that my husband and I agreed on and it gives me a chance to get out a couple of hours in the day. When I am at work it gives me a chance to give the children a rest from me and me a rest from them. But I can't say that I have discovered any mistakes that we may have made in this deal.

Q. What conflicts if any have you had with your husband concerning your effort to combine mothering and work or general family life and work? Were you able to resolve these conflicts?

A. There wasn't really any conflict. It was simply a matter of coming to an agreement, because I spoke to him and I told him that I would really like to go back to work. And I must add too, one reason that I wanted to continue to work and keep up to date with the type of work that I'm doing is that there is no guarantee that he is going to be around forever. God forbid that anything should happen, but if he got sick I would be able to go back to work and earn a decent salary without having to depend on someone else to help us out. That is one of the reasons, one of my main reasons, for continuing to work year in and year out. I like to keep myself up to date with my working habits and routine, so that should an emergency arise I will be able to deal with it.

Q. Yes. So this work is partly for your own sense of security?

A. Yes, to a certain extent.

Q. Do you feel when you look at your own family and work situation that you've been very lucky? That is to say do you know of many other women who just haven't been able to work out a happy arangement for one reason or another? If so, why haven't they, do you think?

A. I think that I am very lucky to have my plans work out as they have, because being able to work gives me the opportunity to do many things that I probably couldn't do if I didn't work. Although the things are not that important, it gives me just that little extra something to do, a few extra things that I wouldn't ordinarily be able to do. I do know of other cases where young mothers want to work but they have been unable to work. First of all, they can't find anyone to keep the children when they are small. Then they have the problem if they find a sitter of not being able to find someone in the neighborhood. If they have to transport the children uptown or across town, its hard. It is easier in the spring and when the weather is nice, but in the winter when there's snow and so much rain it's difficult. Especially, if they have to do this on their own. Most husbands usually leave for work earlier than the wife and if she is going to work she usually tries to arrange her hours so that they are the regular working hours, 9 to 5, or somewhere in that line. If the husband has already gone to work, that means that she has to get up and prepare breakfast, get the children dressed and try to get them to wherever she's going to take them, by herself. And in most cases I know, the mother's usually the one who has to pick up the children in the afternoon, too. If you put in five or six hours and have had to take the children to the sitter and pick them up in the afternoon, prepare dinner, get them ready for bed, etc., by the end of the day you are so tired that maybe you begin to feel sorry that you started this in the first place. But then there are cases of working mothers who have to work, so that's a different case. If they have to work, then the only thing they can do is try to make the best of it.

Q. Do you know of many other husbands who don't like their wives to work or would rather see them stay home? Do you think this is a common husband-wife struggle?

A. Yes, in my particular circle most of the husbands don't want their wives to work. In one or two of the cases it is necessary that the wife work in order to make ends meet, so there is no alternative but for her to get a job. But the majority of my friends and the people that I know mostly don't want their wives to work. I think some husbands seem to feel that once a wife starts to work she gets a certain amount of independence about her which they usually don't want her to feel. I don't feel that way and I don't think my husband feels that way either, because there is a certain amount of independence that everyone should have. If you can cope with this the right way, I don't think there should be any conflict.

Q. In other words some husbands feel a little bit threatened by the whole thing.

A. Yes, because as I said before, in my particular circle there are a lot of the wives who if they were working full-time would probably bring in more money than the husbands.

Q. Do you think as time goes on that husbands are just going to have to adapt to a different kind of wife than they've looked for in the past? In other words, more women are going to want to work and men are going to have to change their attitude about this?

A. I believe that's what is going to happen. I certainly feel that the men are going to have to change their attitude because I find that more women than ever are working. In a sense it's better this way, because if both of them are working there is no conflict in the home as far as money is concerned. It helps both of them because they can achieve whatever they are trying to achieve much faster. If both of them are working, it helps them to get the things that they want.

Q. If more women do start working, will husbands feel so guilty or so bothered if their wife works?

A. The more women that work, the more men will feel different. If for instance, two or three of my girlfriends are working then their husbands will say, if Betty is working, then why not my wife? And why shouldn't she work if this is what she wants to do? I think when more women work it changes the whole attitude toward the working mother.

7

ROSEMARY RUETHER

Reflections of a Nonworking Mother (Smile When You Say That, Partner)

Rosemary Reuther, now in her thirties, has three degrees, including a doctorate in theology, and three school-age children. She teaches several courses at a university, writes books and articles, but refuses to call these activities "work." She sees her "career" as an "extension of herself," and has no sense that these activities conflict with her family life. As an academic activist committed to the inner city and peace, she includes her children in her activities.

I belong to a minority group. It is called "women." Now this is a funny sort of minority group, because it makes us slightly over fifty percent of the total population. But its minority status apparently is created, not by numbers, but by self-consciousness. The creation and reenforcement of this depressing self-consciousness takes ever new forms. Today sociologists, journalists, popular pundits of all

kinds are hard at work renewing this minority self-consciousness by their relentless pursuit of special feelings,
experiences, and attitudes presumed to be "feminine."
Any woman who does not feel at home in this form of
ghetto-think, of course, is merely "hiding something."

The analysis of her trouble is undertaken by reducing
her to the lowest common denominator. In fact, one
doesn't even have to know anything about her individually
to be an expert in analyzing her "trouble." "Total self-
giving" demand the religious moralists; "penis envy"
smirk their Freudian understudies; these sorts of phrases
will do to put that girl in her place without any further
ado. One always deals with girls like that by way of reduc-
tionism. By leveling the individual to the general and
reducing "spirit" to "matter," all rights of proper person-
hood can be silenced. The experts in this science of women
claim, it is true, to be defending the "rights" of this minority person, but the rights which they vindicate always feel
like new shackles. When one author summons all his
imagination to the task of "appreciating" women and
granting their "rights" to compete with him in the academic market place, he somehow manages simultaneously
to imply their probable incompetence to do so. It all somehow comes back to a picture of a creature who is better off
where she belongs, and we all know ahead of time where
that is.

I am not interested in this pseudo-science and have
never read anything on the subject of "women" (or written anything for that matter) which I didn't consider
extremely tedious. The subject of "women" is necessarily
tedious because it is a pseudo-reality, and hence can only
be discussed in the form of general bombast. One must
artificially try to abstract some commonality of experience
where none actually exists. The reductionist nature of
this science of "women" can be readily seen by the fact

that no one would ever think of trying to create a parallel science of "men." Man is simply identical with "human," but "woman" is a subspecies of "human." All science of women operates on this basic assumption. As soon as one denies this basic assumption and asserts that "woman" like man is simply identical with human, the possibility of writing on woman as a special topic disappears. This is why I do not intend to discuss this topic any further. When asked to write books on "women's nature," one should politely refuse. Getting women to write on being women is a part of the trap of permanent ghettoization. One has to learn to recognize patronization for what it is. Once, when asked to do a book on the "theology of women," I firmly replied that there was no such thing, and therefore I could not write on such a topic.

There is no feminine nature, but there is, to be sure, a sociological reality of woman fixed by a long tradition of biological necessity and institutionalized prejudice. And, therefore, there is an interest in how one gets out of this prejudice and undercuts this biological necessity. Catholics particularly are interested in this because they are especially guilty of confirming this prejudice and enforcing this biological necessity. Consequently women who slip through the net are something of a phenomenon, and there is a certain combination of honest interest and morbit curiosity as to "how she did it." So I have undertaken here to discuss how I "as a woman" make it in the "real world," combining "work" with "domesticity." But surely this is a very silly thing to discuss, and I have a hard time taking the question seriously. When ladies at tea-parties give me that glassy-eyed stare (tinged with suspicion) and ask "but what do you *do* with your children," I reply lightly, "oh, I just put them out on the freeway to play." I mean, really, what do they expect? What does anyone *do* with their children? Children are for dressing, washing, handing peanut butter sandwiches to for breakfast, yelling at when you are tired, tickling, laughing and general lolling around. That is what you do with children.

Perhaps I should start by telling about "my day." In the morning I drink a lot of coffee to get my blood back up to par. Over breakfast I glance over my notes for the morning lecture. Today it is "Christological and Iconoclastic Controversies in the East." Then we all discover that it is fifteen minutes later than we thought it was, and rush off in different directions to various institutions of learning. Mimi (age four) goes to a Montessori nursery school in a Jewish Synagogue. David (age seven) goes to a public school which is almost entirely non-Caucasian. Becky (age nine) takes the bus to Catholic University. Herc, my husband, goes west to American University (Methodist), and I go east to Howard University. Having made the scene in most available varieties of school systems, we go through our various paces. At noon most of us come home again for lunch. Then everybody leaves again but myself and Mimi. Mimi colors and plays, and I read. Sometimes I read in warm baths. I also think and write. Thinking and writing also takes place in various postures. I do a lot of cleaning while I am thinking. Think, think (scrub, scrub), type, type, type. Warm baths are another good place for thinking and writing. When I am writing well, I do a lot of cleaning and take many warm baths. I also do a fair amount of thinking and writing while I am cooking, although this is a more complicated combination, and I regret to say that I do burn pots, and there are occasional moments of absent-mindedness, like the time I misplaced a book I was consulting and found it sometime later in the ice box.

Dinner time comes, and we push Herc's books, papers, and typewriter to one side on the dining room table and crowd around the other end. After this everyone cleans up together. The children do their homework, fight, watch TV, and drift off to bed. Herc continues to read on into the early hours of the morning. I put the finishing touches on the next day's lectures and sack in. Sometimes if I have more to do, I rise at 3:00 or 4:00 in the morning to study some more. I do some of my best work in the early hours of the morning.

How do I manage to "work"? That depends on how you define work. "Work" is vacuuming; something I do very sparingly. Leisure is giving lectures on "Christological and Iconoclastic Controversies in the East." I have a lot of leisure, and I don't do much work. I read Haller's book on seventeenth-century Puritanism today in the bath, but that didn't really seem like work, unless one is so shallow-minded as to find seventeenth-century Puritans uninteresting. It is difficult for me to find that part of my daily activities which can be called "my work," because there is really no such special activity which can be disentangled from the pattern of our lives in general. When I am teaching a class, it is not a special activity which I do as "work," but is simply one extension of what I am. Other extensions of what I am include children, houses, reading, writing, running a catechetical program for an Episcopal church, making banners to carry on peace marches and illegal liturgical processions, standing in front of St. Matthew's Cathedral to beg money for the victims of war in North Vietnam, and attending diverse sit-ins, cook-outs, and small riots. It is a variegated life, and usually gives me enough to do. I am a lazy individual and inclined to do things the easy way. I have never felt so rushed that I couldn't waste a fair amount of time in idle chatter or spend an evening lying on the floor with Becky, David, and Mimi watching "Pollyanna."

For some of these activities I get paid, and this helps to finance other activities for which I do not get paid. I had a housekeeper once, but fired her, because I could get more done without her. I seldom have babysitters any more, although when the children were little, a friend with children of parallel ages took care of them in the mornings. It was more a shared family arrangement then hired "babysitting," however. My children have an antipathy to the little-old-lady hired babysitter, and the one or two times I have employed such, they have driven them rapidly from the house. My children are very firm about this, and only will stay with people that they like to stay with anyway. Now the children are rather self-sufficient, and either come along on whatever activities we are doing (they are old hands at picketing public and ecclesiastical strongholds), or else have something better of their own to do. We are very bigoted against the suburbs and insist on living in the center city, and so schools, jobs and home are kept in close proximity. So that's about all I have to say on the subject of "work" and "domesticity."

But, Rosemary, you were supposed to write 3000 very solemn words on this weighty subject? Surely you can come across with something more than that. How did it all start? When did you decide to read books on Puritans in the bath and give lectures on Christological and-so-forth? Surely you must have had to reflect *carefully* on your decision to give your life to these pursuits rather than more womanly endeavors, such as reading *Ladies Home Journal* in the bath and giving lectures on pornography and juvenile delinquency to the Mother's Sodality? Well, actually, no. You see, I never really wanted to read *Ladies Home Journal* and give lectures on pornography and juvenile delinquency anyway. But giving lectures on pornography and juvenile delinquency is so feminine and giving lectures on Christological what-ever-it-was is so unfeminine. Surely you wanted to be feminine, didn't you? Hmmmm. That's a distinction I find hard to follow. Let's bracket the feminine line and just talk about the funny way people grow up and form their pattern of life.

Some years ago I was a little girl. I suppose I was a rather solitary little girl, although I wasn't aware of it at the time. My father died when I was about twelve. My two sisters were somewhat older, and I spent a lot of time just "exploring" and thinking by myself. I grew up in a tall old house that had belonged to my great-grandfather, Admiral Radford, in Georgetown. Georgetown is the old part of Washington that goes back to colonial times. Now it is very elegant, but when I grew up there it was more what we called "shabby genteel." The Radford family comes from Southern gentry of Virginia and Mississippi. They are a little "Faulkneresque" in their native habitat. They are Anglicans, traditionally belong to the vestry of Christ Church, Georgetown, and consider Roman Catholicism an unfortunate myopia. Their wives belong to the Colonial Dames and regard the DAR as relative upstarts. My mother's side of the family were descended from an English Catholic clan that had remained proudly Papist when all about them was becoming Anglican or Puritan. Other than this accomplishment, their religion sat with them lightly. The Ords are a military clan, have many swords hanging around their homes, have a keen memory for family geneologies, and send their sons to West Point if possible. Both sides of my family are a little crazy, in the manner of people who remember too much history. They believe in ghosts, sometimes talk to them, and boast several haunted ancestral homes.

As children we were encouraged to develop an *amour propre*. We were given to understand that, though "poor," we were "well born," and expected to "amount to something." Our family motto, as we all knew, was *possunt quia posse videntur* (which was supposed to mean, for those who can't decipher Radford-latin, "those can who think they can"). All this was well designed to produce people given at once to defensiveness and secret pride, assured of their innate superiority, but needing to prove it by a certain show of swashbuckling self-sufficiency. I might say, however, that this was directed more toward fields of personal endeavor. Nobody ever took the church so seriously in my family as to feel any need to rebel against it. The Southern side of my family didn't expect girls to amount to much, it is true, but this attitude was all but negated in my own case by the general assumption that "those can who think they can" and "a Radford (Ord) can do anything." So much for the formation of my character.

I was a bookworm from my earliest years, although in high school I also did a lot of painting, and cherished a dream of being an "artist." In college, however, other interests crowded out this ambition. I attended a woman's college surrounded by a high wall, planted with long shady walks and rose gardens and graceful ruins of classical and Oriental sculpture. The intellectual atmosphere could be described as an effort to recapture the mystique of the "renaissance man," or in this case the "renaissance woman." We went in strictly for the "big picture." Large ideas were our stock-in-trade: not just any recent ideas, but classical, well-pedigreed ideas. For four years I was mostly immersed in Plato, Aristophanes, and the declensions of the Greek verb. I hardly ever read a newspaper, and I seldom got within shouting distance of the 20th century. My mind hovered like a blissful butterfly over the poppy fields of ancient Greece and Rome.

When I was a junior I met a fellow named Herc (short for Herman) Ruether who read other kinds of books, like

Political Parties in Urban America. His family didn't have any swords or ghosts. His father and uncle came to this country in the 1920s from Pappenburg, Germany, with the skills of carpentry and house painting and $20 to split between them. He read newspapers. We got married, lived in a little house on our joint scholarships, read our books and wrote our papers together, and gradually I began to catch up on society, religion, and politics in the period after the 5th century. In the course of time we acquired three children. This, however, did not in any way alter our basic life style. Rather we had agreed from the beginning that we should continue the good life of perpetual study indefinitely. Consequently I never discontinued going to school, getting scholarships, writing papers, and taking courses, and so by the time I had accumulated three children, I had also acquired three degrees as well. It seems like that was about enough of both, and it was time for a little serious money-making. We both began to teach. This is the way one continues to be a perpetual student after the scholarships have run out.

My first "real" teaching job was in the History Department at Immaculate Heart College, Los Angeles. At least this was where I was supposed to teach. But then things got complicated. Herc was in India at this time doing research. I was intending to spend the latter part of the summer in Mississippi doing civil rights work. Needing a spot of ready cash, I taught Western Civilization in the summer session at the college. Pocketing my check, and sending the kiddies off to Grandmother's for six weeks at the beach, I departed to lend my hand to the revolution. When I returned Los Angeles had experienced a bigger revolution. The local Catholic diocese was shaking with its tempest in a teapot. By some concatenation of events I found my academic status very much in "limbo" in the midst of all this. Certain things I had written about civil rights and the "Cardinal" were not too well liked. Also I had done a few pieces of writing on birth control which some people seemed to find "offensive to pious ears." The Immaculate Heart Sisters, however, are fairly skilled players of the game of "non grata" and found a way to hide me amid the folds of their institutional robes. However, instead of teaching Western Civilization to 18-year-olds, I found myself teaching theology to novices! The credibility gap was almost too marvelous. Being too dangerous (vis-à-vis the chancery) to teach history to lay students, instead I taught Reformation theology to prospective sisters.

It was kind of a fun year, but not something one would want to repeat. I got a little tired of jokes about "coming to Immaculate Heart from Claremont *via* the underground railway." I couldn't get used to the deviousness, the persecution complex, the inability to face up to issues directly which seemed to be the means of survival in the Catholic world. It didn't really seem worth surviving on those terms. So it was something of a relief to know that we would be moving from Los Angeles the following year.

In looking for new jobs, one might ask, "Who comes first: you or Herc?" The answer quite simply is, both of us together. But we look for his job first because his "career" is more in his job than mine. But we look for a job for him in places that also offer opportunities for me. One-college towns, places without good libraries, in fact, I would say, "little places" are out. We had several suitable offers, but the best combination was found in Washington with Herc teaching at the Centre for South and South-East Asian Studies of the American University and I at the School of Religion at Howard University. I teach a lecture course in the early period of Church

History and seminars in Historical Theology and Contemporary Radical Theology. Next semester I am developing a course called "Theology of Social Change." I usually try to teach whatever it is that I want to read at the time, and so far I have succeeded fairly well.

I am also doing a lot of writing for magazines and journals, and more and more am being asked to give talks and even sermons(!) at various universities. These sidelines have snowballed in a somewhat humorous way from an accidental beginning. I suppose I always thought I would do some publishing, but on obscure academic topics like "the twilight of the Homeric gods." But it seemed that the twilight of other gods were pending. It began over this silly business of birth control. I had never bought the party line on birth control anyway, and presumed that after we had finished having about three children, something "serious" would have to be done. But I must confess that I hadn't given the matter a great deal of thought. I sort of drifted along, adapting my schedule to eventualities. I took my qualifying exams for the Ph.D. a few weeks before Mimi arrived in the world, and was well decided to use contraceptive pills in the future, which my Jewish doctor assured me were quite safe. I was annoyed by the church's attitudes, and as I thought about it further I became more annoyed. It was not that I needed any "permission" to do anything, since my own attitude on the church's teaching was determined years before I was even married. But the stupidity and effrontery of the whole Catholic ethos was humiliating. However, I probably would have been content to vindicate my *arete* by smashing a few priests verbally to the floor had not an incident occurred in the hospital that stirred my spleen to greater heights of argumentation.

There was a Mexican woman in the bed next to me named Assumptione who was having her ninth child. The

child was born with a twisted body. Assumptione be-
moaned long and often the miserable condition of her
home, the lack of heat, her fear of turning on the stove
because of the leaking gas, and finally this child who
seemed doomed to a permanent deformity. Yet she was
fatalistically resigned to returning to the hospital each
year to have yet another child. Her doctor several times
tried to impress on her the need for birth regulation, but
she threw up her hands, wept, and sighed "the priest, he
tells my husband 'no'; he say, he won't let us come to
church." I got mad. I got very, very mad. I got so mad
that when I got home I began to write many things to
all kinds of places. I had to figure out all kinds of arguments—philosophical, sociological, psychological—which
had not occurred to me previously because I had not
needed them before. I read up on the formations of the
foe, and plotted his overthrow. I also learned to write
"emotionally," something which was foreign to my previous training. Soon I had quite a knack for writing what
I call "the bleeding mother piece." Not that this was
insincere. There were the real dilemmas, but one creates
weapons suitable to the nature of the task. As it turned
out, the time was exactly ripe for such an attack, and the
avalanche came down by removing only one or two
pebbles. Lots of other things began to come down about
the same time. I found myself, to my surprise, a famous
(infamous) "writer." Soon people wanted me to write
books on "birth control" and "women," and I had to ex-
plain that I was only a talented amateur, and this really
wasn't my "field." Once one gets swimming around in
that journalistic pond, however, it's hard to get out. Soon
I found myself in full howl with all those other eager
hounds on the scent of "what is wrong with the church."
One thing leads to another, and the more you try to

clarify things, the deeper in you get. I suppose now I will be trying to figure out what is wrong with the church for the rest of my life, although I must say that I have nostalgic moments when I wish I could go back to writing about Dionysius and Apollo and other such gods whose priesthoods and colleges of cardinals have long since left the scene.

These few reflections on my "life and hard times" don't really have much to do with the feminine angle, but as I explained before I find it hard to say anything longer than two paragraphs on that subject. Let me just sum up my approach however. I have a delightful family, a house full of books, and a mind teeming with lots of ideas which spin me off in various directions. It is a good life. But I do not "work," I don't have a "double career" (schizophrenic life), and I don't "leave the home" to pursue a profession (unless any physical displacement from the four walls of the house, i.e., going to the market, is classed as "leaving the home"). I don't share the premises from which these kinds of phrases arise. What I do is to pursue a leisure culture very much on my own terms. I don't happen to believe in the puritan work culture. I believe in getting through the basic necessities of survival as simply as posible and using the rest of your energies to cultivate the good life. Teaching, writing, thinking, lecturing is a part of leisure, not work. For some of this I happen to get paid, but this basically covers the expense of leisure itself, and the value of what I do is not determined by or measured by what I get paid or whether I get paid. In fact, I suspect, that in cultural achievements, pay is in inverse proportion to value. I am fortunate to be a woman, because that makes it easier for me to reject the tyranny of "work."

8

MARY LYNNE BIRD

I'm Glad I've Always Had to Work

Mary Lynne Bird has always worked full-time since her marriage. She has been a teacher, a researcher in the social sciences and part-time professional singer. In her thirties, she now has two school-age children. Married to a graduate student and scholar, her work has been a financial necessity. Yet because of her professional commitment, her work and her urban life style have become a free choice. She has problems of management but no conflicts over combining work and family life.

There have been so many special circumstances that have made job and motherhood compatible for me that I have always been very cautious about suggesting to someone else—on the basis of my experience—that the combination might work for her too. But the benefits derived from continuing to maintain a career after becoming a mother justify at least this brief account. Random factors in my situation could perhaps be more deliberately taken advantage of or programmed into her life style by someone else who is thinking of combining family with career.

Above all, the combination of a professsion with motherhood has been encouraged by a friendly climate. Both my husband and I feel that a wife ought to be able to work if she feels it is right for her in her situation. Both of us come from families in which the attitude toward mothers who have jobs is practical and undogmatic. The general feeling is that if one has to work, one does. Or if one wants to work and it can be managed, fine. On the other hand it is just as admirable to get married and be the compleat housewife ever after. When her children were young my mother worked at various times for a total of about three years. My grandmother went to work when she still had a child under eight years of age, at a time when that was much more unusual than it is today. In sum, we may have analyzed precisely what we think about working mothers a bit more consciously than our parents had cause to do, but attitudes do not differ very much.

As it happens, I would have had to work even if one or both of us had felt differently about it, but the results would have been far less constructive both professionally and personally if either of us had had a hostile attitude toward the whole idea. If there had been resentment over the fact that I worked, the problems of adjustment and accommodation we have had would certainly have been far more serious than they have been, and it is not difficult to imagine some additional ones that would have turned up. But whether I should work or not has seldom come up for discussion either for the present or for the future.

This accepting context has had a strong impact on the

course of my employment. It has meant that when looking for a new job my concern has been with professional
continuity and development as much as with income and
a practical working situation. Obviously that has made
job-hunting vastly more complicated than it is already by
having to take the children's needs into account. It has
taken a great deal of time, energy, and above all in-
genuity to find the kind of job that was right for me each
time I have set out to find a new one. It has meant that
I was obliged to send out numerous resumés, make many
inquiries and contacts, scan catalogs, and write letters to
track down a job that frequently paid little more than a
secretarial job would have. And the latter I could have
found in one day in the classified ad section of the newspaper.

Obviously, this is a great deal of trouble to take, and
there would be no point in bothering if one were not
really professionally oriented. But since this is my bent,
there is a tremendous advantage—well worth the effort—
to staying in my field if only in some peripheral area or
part-time during these years when full professional involvement is impossible. It not only makes the difference
between making at least some limited professional progress
instead of atrophying, but it prevents a shifting self-
concept. Without this continuing contact with the field,
there is much greater likelihood that when the children
are grown I would go back to work at something quite
different. It would be almost impossible to walk back
into the field at that point. The logical thing to do would
be to turn to something less demanding of background
—and to that extent less satisfying and challenging.

It has proved valuable not only to make the effort to
stay in my field but to make the most of being there. Each
job I have held has meant not only that there were certain

assignments to complete and gain information and experience from, but also the opportunity to scan the literature, take note of the people, and keep in touch with what is going on in the field. In the process of doing my assignments, it has not involved much more effort to keep an eye out for things that should be read or checked up on for my own use. It has been a simple matter of maintaining an intellectually acquisitive frame of mind.

Having made the effort to see to it that the work is personally valuable, and being disposed to make the most of its value, I have then in turn found greater motivation to persevere than would have been the case if I had drifted into something that was "just a job."

Necessity has provided not only an impetus but some secondary supports.

Having to be a wage earner has made it unnecessary and irrelevant to defend my career to anyone. This is not to say that I have not chosen on occasion to make a case for the working mother, but I have not had to justify *my* working to people who do not hold the same views I do about careers for women. When a husband's education is not finished, society has almost come to expect that, children or not, one works—and for quite a while. (Didn't the Yale study say that it takes an average of eleven years to get a doctorate in the United States?) Someone critical of working mothers in principle is likely to be more tolerant of a wife working to help put her husband through school.

Immunity to possible criticism has been a pleasant convenience when it involved outsiders, but it has really counted for most within the family. There have certainly been occasions when the children would have preferred to have me stay home and not go off to work. There is little probability that I would have enjoyed much success trying to convince them of what I believe, that in numerous ways it is good for all of us that I go to work regularly. But there can hardly be any lasting protests when we all know that my paycheck is needed too. Admittedly, that hard fact was larded with the value statements that most grownups work, that Mommy enjoys her work the way the children enjoy their projects, and that all of us go out to do things and then come home to be together. They have been willing to accept these ideas intellectually but their subjective reconciliation to the situation is certainly based more on the knowledge that it can not be changed.

As friendly as my husband is to the notion of working wives and mothers, there have been times when he was annoyed enough with the accompanying inconveniences that he would have favored my quitting work for a while at least, if it had been possible. I have occasionally felt the same way. After all there are discouraging times in any undertaking—days when one feels just plain tired, days when it would be very tempting to stay home and take it easy. In that mood, the thought of not having any responsibilities outside the family or any professional deadlines to meet has sometimes been very appealing. Everyone, even the most active person, feels that way once in a while, but it is a temptation that a man seldom has the opportunity to indulge. It may be a mixed blessing that in our society a married woman usually has the option to do precisely that. It has been a generally beneficial discipline for me not to have had the option. Sporadic misgivings about working have been very few. But there is no question that I might have spent time agonizing over whether my decision to work was the most constructive choice if there had been any real possibility of doing anything else.

So much for the personal disposition. Now for some practical details.

The nature of my professional involvement has made it ideal work for a woman with children. Since a few weeks after our first child was born I have (1) worked as a research assistant in either a university or a research foundation, (2) done some independent writing, and, (3) in recent years, done a small but increasing amount of professional singing. Flexibility is common to all three activities—flexibility of place, flexibility of number of hours, and flexibility as to what portion of the day (morning, afternoon, or evening) is involved. A large portion of the work can be done at home. Much of it can be done in the evenings or on weekends as easily as during regular business hours. And pacing of how much is done in a given week or month can be adjusted to some extent to accommodate fluctuating responsibilities at home. Such flexibility is probably the most important criterion in making employment a serious possibility for a mother of young children. Certainly the most serious weakness in the best laid plans for a schedule of regular work away from home is the universal talent of small children for getting sick without warning at the worst possible times. Unless there is an unemployed relative on the scene or some other built-in, instantly available mother-substitute, a woman with children simply cannot punch a time clock regularly, relying on the usual sick leave to cover these emergencies.

As our children have gotten older, a flexible schedule has become even more essential than when they were smaller. Before they were in school, any daytime work away from home required a babysitter. Consequently a reasonably regular schedule of work hours covered by babysitting help had to be established. For the most part, this could be adhered to except on those few occasions when a child was too sick to have anyone else's care but mine. Since they have been in school it has been possible for me to work during school hours without employing a babysitter. But this means that when they are home with a cold or have a holiday, I cannot expect a regularly scheduled sitter to come in and allow me to go out to work as usual. A week which includes several gaps like that can be made up for partly by accomplishing more work in the evenings or during another week with a more fortuitous schedule and sometimes by using sitters on an ad hoc basis whenever they are available. But this all requires some kind of work in which one's presence on a fixed schedule at a particular place away from home is not necessary to get the work done and is not a requirement of the employer.

It has been a matter of great luck for me to be able to find work that can be done on this kind of free schedule, because such jobs are extremely rare. Our economy and society are geared to a large extent to having most people work in a particular place from nine to five. Even when that is not necessary, we are so conditioned to expect it, that most executives and administrators find it difficult to think in terms of the part-time or flexible schedules that could make it possible for more mothers to work. One cannot help but speculate about the possibilities of alleviating the secretarial, nursing, and teaching shortages, for instance, if a few people in high places were more imaginative in making up work schedules.

It might have been difficult to make even such a suitable work schedule function if it were not for the fact that we have only two children and they have been reasonably healthy. There have been no long serious illnesses that required a great deal of maternal care and time-consuming medical visits. There *have* been many long stretches of weeks and even months when there was at least one child sick and shut in. But these illnesses have generally been of the minor type which a babysitter can handle very well. Getting out to work during such a siege has always been especially helpful for both the children and me. A rest from each other after being shut in together for a long time has usually been psychologically therapeutic. It has done the children good to have someone else's company and exercise of authority for a little while after having been with me constantly. And it is amazing how much more patient, objective, and good-natured I have found it is possible to be after being away from the children for a few hours. Frequently when I have been away from the situation for a little while, it has been possible to think through some behavior problem in perspective and return to it with fresh energy and a more certain approach about what I am doing as a mother.

Fortunately, we have not had much cause to be concerned about the influence of outsiders on the children. There have been several reasons for this. Because of the irregularity of my working hours and the amount of work I have done at home and in the evening, the children have never spent a majority of their waking time with a sitter. The impact of any one sitter has further been diluted by the fact that we have almost always used a group of sitters dividing up the sitting-hours among them. We have never kept a sitter whose approach to the children was not basically one that we agreed with. Casual discussions of various things the children have done and how certain problems have been handled have made it easy to spot an attitude or method of managing the children that we did not want to see continued. We could not have managed this luxury of choice and variety if we had not always had a reasonably good supply of sitters to draw on. We have been additionally fortunate in having found many wonderful people among those who have sat for us, people we and the children have enjoyed knowing and who have broadened the children's interests, experience, and outlook on life.

The fact that my husband is an academic and has a very full and unconventional work schedule has been another major factor in making it practical for me to find a variety of available hours for work. If he worked on a nine-to-five schedule and expected to spend evenings and weekends relaxing and socializing, there would be very little time outside of regular weekday working hours that would be free for my work. There probably would not be enough working time to carry on any work of much interest to me. But he is as often absent on weekends or in the evening as in the daytime during the week, and when he is home he spends many hours working. Consequently, it is possible for me to go to the library or out to rehearse or perform in the evening or on weekends. Or we may both spend the evening at home working.

The fact that much of the work I do is a type of work my husband does has been a crucial factor. It has made each of us more aware of and tolerant about the professional demands on the other. The importance of this has been brought home to me when problems have arisen over my singing. Since music is a field in which my husband has not had experience, it is much harder for him to understand and be sympathetic about the way it functions and how one works in it. But he has enjoyed hearing about the writing or research projects I have worked on and has been very patient about the intense activity that has sometimes been brought on by a particular deadline.

He has made helpful suggestions about research techniques or tools and in turn has been vociferously delighted with the random items of value to him that I have found now and then in the course of my work. This sharing of similar professional experiences has had many other complicated and beneficial effects on both our careers and our marriage. It is one of the strongest reasons I have for wanting to work.

There have been a number of fortunate developments which have helped along the way. We had planned that as soon as possible after my husband finished his graduate work I would go back to graduate school to prepare for college teaching, research, and writing. But it was no more than an accident that academic research presented itself as an occupation in the interim. When we were first married, I left graduate school as my husband entered it. I taught school until a few months before our first child was born. I took a clerical job on a university research project. When a vacancy occurred in the research staff, the director shifted me into it. It took only a short time to show us what a difference it would make for me to stay in such academic work, as close to my field as possible. I might have felt quite differently about working at all if I had been shunted off for ten years or so into something completely different and uninteresting to me. The conclusion to draw from this experience would seem to be that one way of creating a non-regimented, interesting job that a woman with children can manage is to take a job in a field in which she has interest and competence even if it is a job for which she is overqualified. A realistic employer encountering such a person in such a situation is probably going to find a way of employing her skills more fully.

The next happy turn came a few weeks after our first

child was born. We moved into a student dormitory as faculty residents at the college where my husband was teaching. The significant feature of the living arrangement for me was that we ate some of our meals in the university dining hall. Seldom having to prepare a dinner for the two years that we were there was an incredibly valuable gift of time and energy.

Living on a college campus also provided us with a ready source of babysitters. Our experience with college girls as sitters has generally been very positive. We have employed older women at times and have found that although they have a tendency to be neater and do more in the way of housework, college girls are more flexible and cheerful and the children have been happier with them. We have also had good success with several young married women. Since our children are used to having had sitters come in regularly since before they can remember, they are accustomed to the idea of having other people care for them part of the time and have seldom objected to having a sitter. They have occasionally not liked a particular sitter. When they have still felt that way after a second session, we have not had the person come back. On the whole they have liked and enjoyed their sitters. And we have been fortunate in always having a rather good supply from which to select. Our children are quite sociable. They are not shy and they enjoy meeting people. Whether this is a result of or a reason for our good babysitting experiences would not be easy to ascertain, but one can assume that the two are related.

We have similarly had good experience with nursery schools. The fact that our children had no more than the usual adjustment problems was an obvious help. Having had more contact with people outside their family than the children of non-working mothers may have contributed to this. Once again, the fact that my working hours could be rearranged was crucial in making the nursery school experience a successful one for all of us. I was able at first to go with the children as much as was necessary to get them happily settled into the school routine and society. The investment of time made at the beginning was well worth the time that was gained later on as each child became accustomed to the school schedule, and we had the satisfaction of knowing that they were not merely being cared for but were enjoying a vital educational and developmental experience. This whole situation would have been far different if time had not been available to get the enterprise under way. If my work schedule had been a fixed one we would have had to settle for more babysitting instead of nursery school which would have been a great loss.

It is doubtful whether any of this would have been possible if we had not always lived in a city and rather close to my place of work. Fortunately, our yearning for the country is usually satisfied by occasional weekend visits or a summer month with relatives. When it gets down to the nitty-gritty of living life, my husband and I are both urban types to the core. We function best in the city, and appealing as the suburbs are for gracious living, the idea of actually trying to carry on our kind of active involvement there is a paralyzing thought.

The advantages of urban living for my holding a job are as important as they are obvious. The more people there are living in a neighborhood, the larger is the pool of potential babysitters to draw from, and the less complicated is the process of getting them from where they live to where we live. There is also a greater age mixture in a city neighborhood. One is less apt to find a situation common to suburban developments of many families with young children in the same neighborhood without the teenagers or older women one usually looks to for baby-sitting.

Even more vitally, city living has meant that it has not been necessary to travel far from home to job. We have found this to be more desirable than living near my husband's work whena choice has had to be made. When he goes to work, he stays until he is finished for the day. Ordinary commuting, while hardly a joy of life, is not a special handicap for him. On the other hand, I must frequently go back and forth between work and home two or three times a day. The typical fragmented day of a wife and mother simply does not allow for much commuting time. When we live three blocks from a library where much of my work can be done, it makes sense to walk there for a couple of hours of work in the evening after the children are in bed. It would not be sensible to do so if an hour's travel were necessary to get there and another hour to get back. If we lived in the suburbs, traveling would waste not only my time but the money we would be paying a babysitter while I was traveling. The result would be that I would probably be forced to find some work near our residence which would undoubtedly mean work out of my field, if indeed there were any work available at all.

This would not be a balanced account if mention were not made of some of the problems that have been caused or aggravated by my being employed.

The difficulty most apparent to anyone who walks into our house is the fact that I have never been able to keep house the way my husband and I would like to have our house kept. It is seldom that the niceties are accomplished and it is not always that the necessities can be counted upon. Nor is it possible to keep up with all the various errands that wives and mothers usually take care of for their husbands, children, households, and themselves. Things get done after a fashion, but usually behind time and then, only when really necessary. Furthermore, they must be done in the quickest way, which is often not the best way.

There is also the matter of fatigue. Whether I actually get less sleep and am more active than other women with children who do not have jobs, or whether the pressure of trying to balance and meet so many responsibilities is the really tiring factor, it would be difficult to say. But it does seem to me frequently that I am more tired than I care to be.

It is apparent to me that these problems would be considerably minimized if I were working only by choice and could use a substantial part of my income to pay for help. It has seemed to me that if I did not have to work and at the same time manage most of a housewife's normal activities on my own, most of these problems would magically vanish. But this may be an appealing delusion. Perhaps these are liabilities that are built into the combination of working while keeping house and caring for a family. It may be that no amount of hired help could substantially alleviate these problems.

One last complication that should be mentioned is the effect of my work on the juggling of our family's social calendar. Most couples undoubtedly plan visits, cultural events, and recreation around the husband's professional commitments. In our household my work and appointment calendar must be taken into account as well as my husband's when events involving both of us are planned. Since there are often conflicts that mean missing some event my husband would like to have attended, I have increasingly refrained from involving us in activities of

my choice, so that when we do go out or entertain, it is
something he chooses or feels we should do. This has
somewhat minimized unnecessary aggravation of an in-
eradicable problem. My husband has probably shown
more conscious tolerance on this point than any other
difficulty resulting from my working, except perhaps my
housekeeping.

These are not trivial problems. Many women would not
feel that working would be worth these difficulties, or,
even more likely, their husbands would not think it was.
I can only state with deep conviction that (1) it has been
worth it to me and my family and that (2) my husband
has encouraged me at each step of the way. He has said
that he would find it as difficult to be married to a full-
time housewife as I would find it to be one. I am sure
(because I have met some) that there are women whose
personalities and situations permit them to manage growth
and engagement of the same kind while being full-time
housewives and mothers. But I am not one of them. I
would find it almost impossible under the guise or impetus of "keeping up" to take the time away from husband, household, and children to read the book or article
or go to the library or lecture that professional commitment impels me to do now. Without my having a job, my
husband would undoubtedly urge me to do those things—
even at the expense of the same activities that get slighted
now. But my feelings about priorities would be far more
complicated than they are in the situation of meeting the
demands of professional employment. Direct and immediate responsibilities exert a much stronger pressure on
my sense of obligation than indirect ones no matter how
firm my recognition of their validity might be. When I
feel I *should* make time for some activity, it is not so apt
to get done as when I *must* do it. It seems reasonable to

suppose that there are a number of other women who react similarly. Surely there are many other husbands who get exasperated about that fact and who would be quite willing to have their wives work to insure a certain amount of continuing alertness and intellectual growth commensurate with their own.

This situation represents both an enormous cumulative individual need and an intriguing social possibility. One could construct an impressive set of statistics projecting the woman-hours which could be made available to our economy under the proper conditions—works-hours which in all probability would funnel for the most part into those sectors where there is a long-standing and increasing labor shortage.

A positive climate of opinion about working mothers has developed far ahead of practical measures to increase their number and improve their lot and that of their families. The most immediate and easily accomplished step would be to break down more jobs into part-time— and, whenever possible—flexible work schedules. Even without added child-care facilities, this in itself would enable additional millions of women to hold jobs or to hold them more happily than is now possible. Undoubtedly, many married women without children would also prefer such jobs if they could get them.

The most significant measure, however, would be the massive formation of a variety of child-care facilities. A number of private businesses have experimented successfully with company-run nursery schools, operated at cost. The proliferation of such enterprises would draw women into the business world. But to channel women into jobs in the public sector government would have to go into the child-care business. Since there is an even greater need for women's services in this area, it would be an investment worth making. The evidence from those child-care systems which already exist here and abroad shows that fees charged by schools which plan to break even financially are still low enough to make it sensible for large numbers of mothers to work. Therefore, although government *initiative* would definitely be necessary, government *subsidy* would not have to continue—unless there were a deliberate effort to link such a plan to the poverty program and encourage mothers of poor families to work by offering lower nursery-school rates to them.

For all kinds of sociological and economic reasons the trend in the United States is for more mothers to enter the job market. I think their response is the right one. My question is whether society will provide the right response to them.

9

JEAN CAMPER CAHN

Maximum Feasible Participation from Everybody

Jean Camper Cahn is in her thirties and a black lawyer noted for her creativity and social concern. She is married to a prominent lawyer and has two young school-age sons. Combining motherhood with law school and a highly demanding career has been hectic but rewarding. Mrs. Cahn has tried to include her children in her "crisis-oriented" law practice whenever it was possible.

My oldest son Jonathan made his appearance in the Cahn household on the first day of scheduled exams my first year at Yale Law School. With the same unerring and "prophetic" sense of timing, Reuben arrived 16 months later when Edgar and I were studying in England at Cambridge University. Edgar and I made no decisions about whether "to combine or not to combine" a career with motherhood. The children came . . . we attempted to survive.

Reuben's favorite childhood phrase was "I do it my-self." Sometimes, however, it got second billing to "may it please the court" (accompanied by the rhythmic clank-ing of a tablespoon on his highchair). He caught the es-sence of our existence in those phrases as well as in the bifurcated contracted noun "mama-da" applied indiscrim-inately to Edgar and myself.

Our financial condition was such that the public hous-ing project in New Haven told us we were ineligible because we didn't have enough money. Pembroke College, Cambridge, emerging from their state of shock that we were not rich Americans, gave me a scholarship and brought care packages. However, when things really got bad—like a two thousand dollar hospital bill—stubborn old Edgar allowed my parents to pull us out of the hole.

The months after Jonathan's birth will never be for-gotten. A typical day looked like this. Six A.M. feeding for Jonathan (he was breast fed). He was probably the first exponent of a "feed-in." A minimum of 45 minutes was required. At the end of an hour and a half, I fixed his 10 o'clock bottle (oh agonies of fullness from that bottle at 10). Breakfast for Edgar and myself. Make beds, stack dishes, fold diapers, somehow catch the bus at 10 minutes to 9 for my first class at 9:10. Class until 12. We paid a neighbor to come in to help three days a week. On the other days I rushed home, gave Jonathan his 2 o'clock feeding, and went back to school for an afternoon semi-nar. Sometimes Jonathan came back with me to sleep in the registrar's office or to crawl around in the library.

The evening found me scurrying to fix dinner, nursing Jonathan while I attempted to eat and, finally, rocking the carriage with one foot, standing on the other, one hand in the dishpan, and the other turning the pages of the constitutional law casebook.

Aware that Edgar was suffering, I, of course, did my best. Edgar woke me up one night to tell me that in a valiant, last ditch attempt at brightness, charm, and companionship I had sat up in bed, smiled and asked, "Are you in interstate commerce?" (He had just come home from the 5 o'clock factory shift—one of the two full-time jobs he held down while in graduate school).

The next years were filled with measles, mumps, flu, and what our pediatrician once referred to as "Lake Place Crud." All childrens' diseases exhausted, we both finished school (Edgar, after getting a Ph.D. in English, completed Yale Law School) and moved to Washington, D.C. By this time, the children had undergone four graduations. The first for Jonathan was "sans sa mere." (No wonder I instinctively understood the Rule Against Perpetuities in my Future Interests class.)

It was equally foreordained that Jonathan would conclusively sum up that whole period of our existence in a story: "The Potato That Went to College" which he wrote by saying to the housekeeper "take this down" (imitating my method of working in the best State Department fashion). This potato did everything that he had seen in New Haven—aspired to get knowledge, left the farm, went to the big city, worked hard, got good grades, graduated with distinction—and then decided to go back and tell the other potatoes about the wonders of education. That, noted Jonathan qua author, was his "big mistake." For when he went back to Farmer Brown's, he was bagged with all the other potatoes. And the story ended. "So just think, when you eat potatoes, you may be eating the potato that went to college." So much for the enduring values of higher education!

Leaving our helper Aunt Mott-Mott behind, we now commenced a new phase in our career and a new kind of travail. All help in Washington seems to come from South Carolina. Sandwiched between unworkable South Carolinian maids was a Swedish maid who used hair spray to remove the stains and smell left by Tuffy, our untrainable dog; a really excellent maid from Maryland, who turned out to be a registered nurse dropped from the register because of dope addiction; and one massive 6-foot 2-inch 250-pound matron whom I decided was incompetent when she came in one Monday morning with two black eyes she had acquired from her 5-foot 4-inch 130-pound boyfriend. Live-in, live-out, they were nothing but trouble.

Finally we hit upon an idea. Why not hire a live-out maid (a cut above the live-in ones) and have an *au pair* like when we were in England. Being true Americans, we adapted the *au pair* system rather than adopted it. And of course our adaptation had the great virtue of not costing the usual $300-$400 for transportation. After a two day stint with a frail little Japanese girl whom we ended up waiting on, we advertised for a male foreign student. The men worked out wonderfully except that the juvenile atmosphere already prevalent in the house was now overwhelming.

Today in Washington our day looks like this. The children get up with our student and theoretically he supervises their dressing. Then they cook their own breakfast and gather books together. We get up, dress, gulp a quick cup of coffee, and the children are off to school. Actually, 15 minutes after they're awake, Reuben rushes into our room to get us to referee the wrestling match in their bedroom.

"Is your hair brushed?" "Did you wash your teeth?" "Pick those dirty clothes off the floor!" "If you don't hurry you'll be late." Ever forward goes the monologue until at last they are out the door. By now, of course, my husband has left to catch his 8:00 plane. These trips take place with great regularity—twice a week at 7:45 A.M. Its not that he's commuting with regularity to the same place on the same plane. Its simply part of the conspiracy to generally cause chaos and confusion in the Cahn home.

Then to the office. Read the morning mail, review cases, set up priorities with my research assistant, and then, if I am lucky, down to serious work. But that's not the way it usually goes. Somebody else's client calls or one of mine panics or three or four or five people "just happened to be passing by." That's what one means by having the office conveniently located.

Provided things are calm, we get home by 6:45. With the children already fed, we can review homework, discuss problems, cut hair, listen to violin lessons, and they are off to bed at 8:30. That, from my point of view, is the ideal day.

I do not handle the estates, wills, and domestic problems usually relegated to my female counterparts. My practice for the most part is "crisis oriented." You must be prepared if you're going to court in the morning or trying to squeeze a client's program under the wire of the current fiscal year. You must be prepared even if it means not going home, staying up all night, and keeping extra sets of clothes in the office.

When most lawyers are in trouble, they call in experts. When I'm in trouble I call in the children. During one office crises which continued from January to April, 1967, Reuben collated briefs, Jonathan became my dynamo clipping service, and my husband pitched in on the after-midnight research. I think that it was despair which finally led Jonathan to snitch my constitutional law casebook to read *Marshall* v. *Taney* to find out whether I was really on the right track. "Maximum feasible participation" in the Cahn family was finally carried to a ridiculous extreme when the children sent a letter to my client telling him that he had better handle the case himself because he was, and I quote, "smarter than all his lawyers." Oh my aching hairbrush!

I've never been certain whether it was a coup d'etat or a surrender when the children held their own trial on the validity of an IOU which my male *au pair* had given them. Whatever it was, they held court three days with their own version of "discovery" procedures, depositions, and equity.

Of course it hasn't been all fun and games. My career affects quite seriously the lives of the other members of the family. And despite my absolute relish of the practice of law, I too, often suffer from involvment in my profession. While I believe combining a career, a marriage, and a family makes me a better wife and mother, there are costs paid by all of us—not just money, but tension, hurts, crises, and setbacks which leave wounds that heal slowly and leave permanent scars.

Of course, the children love being trotted to the Navajo reservation, California, Puerto Rico, Massachusetts, and elsewhere when professional demands require my absence from home for fairly long stretches. The expenditures to take them, continue to pay home expenses, employ a babysitter at our destination so as to be free for business, while costly, are not regretted. I do find pause in wondering about the damage this sporadic uprooting does to their schooling, but more important, what it does to their relationships with their schoolmates. Sometimes when there are particular problems with which I feel I need to deal, I must forego scrutiny of them until my professional obligations are lighter. The planning for birthday parties is often worked out in taxis to court or sandwiched between interviews with clients. Praise be to those stores that stay open until midnight and on Sunday!

In the grey world of professionalism, deviation is usually regarded as the cardinal sin. Being a woman is in itself a deviation of mammoth proportions. But a black woman, a Jewish woman, and a woman in the private practice of law constitutes a galaxy of sins of gargantuan proportion. So I am "thrice" damned . . . but at least free to continue to sin. The totality of being a woman who is a black, Jewish mother and wife who practices law perhaps can be summed up in the following way.

How does it affect being a mother? Well . . . one day Jonathan, who was at that time seven years old, came home with this story. I had sent him to school with a note requesting that the teacher excuse his absence on the previous day because it was Yom Kippur—a Jewish holiday. The teacher told him to stand in the corner because she intended to punish him for an unexcused absence. He replied he had an excuse, he was home for the holiday. According to her the absence was not excused because it wasn't his holiday. It couldn't be. He was a Negro (and he didn't have a patch over one eye). Oh yes, she had seen my note. But quite obviously it confirmed her growing impression that my son and I were conspiring against the sacrosanct rules of the school. And so the "Oh-yes-you-did, no-I-didn't" dispute continued until Jonathan (inspired) responded that under the circumstances he wasn't going to be punished because she had no evidence and he had had no trial. Outraged, she tried harder. Further inspired, Jonathan protested (now being pushed from the room by his teacher) that his Mommy had told him that there was a piece of paper in Washington which said no one could be punished until he had a trial. For that he was rewarded by a trip to the principal's office. But there he sought and obtained vindication.

The children pay a price for my sins. This very incident would never have escalated into such a conflict if Jonathan's innate sense of fairness—the sense all children have—had not been reinforced by the fixed belief that somehow the law and constituted authority will stand behind those instincts and protect them. The cost of such a belief may be increased conflict, but the rewards may be a protection of what is most precious and most easily destroyed in a child, the thing that ultimately shapes his character and his moral fiber.

How does the totality affect being a wife? Another incident may suffice to tell that story. A certain high government official, having just gone to New Haven during the riots, sought to drag Edgar and myself from our Vermont vacation. Thinking the situation urgent, we called and went over to see him at his house our first night back in the city. He told his tale of horror, lamented that simply no one on the riot commision had any understanding of those rioting blacks, and, he said, they (not the rioters, but the commissioners) needed help. Looking earnestly at me and my husband sitting side by side on the couch, he said intensely, "That's why I told them to get in touch with you, Edgar, because you could really give them insight." And I felt my husband's white hand tremble ever so slightly over my black one and saw him just barely control that oh-so-wicked, crooked, Jewish smile of his. Let us hope that I never cease to be amused by White America!

And what does all of this mean in my capacity as my husband's colleague? Most of the work for which my husband and I are known, both in this country and abroad, has been joint work—as a result of articles co-authored and speeches which are joint presentations. The problem I face as a "co-worker" is illustrated by an incident which occurred recently. Some professors at George Washington University Law School discussed with my husband the possibility of his heading a graduate program for VISTA lawyers. This requires knowledge and skill in both poverty law and community organization, fields which are the direct outgrowth of techniques I developed in New Haven as the first "neighborhood" lawyer in the United States and later in Washington as the founder of the legal service program for the national anti-poverty agency. My husband responded that he was committed to his present job. Edgar replied to a requisition for suggestions that the only person he knew who was really qualified was his wife, Jean. Since I must assume these professors are among the more sophisticated, knowledgeable men in the area of poverty law, their response stunned me—they asked Edgar if I had any "qualifications" separate from his.

Edgar, while admitted to both the Connecticut and D.C. Bars, has never had occasion to practice law. I, on the other hand, have been continually in active practice, with the exception of a year divided between the State Department and the national poverty agency. Not only do I have experience in teaching law but I also have training and experience in community organization. While all of this is clearly set forth in each of our joint publications, people automatically attribute my qualifications to my husband—but not vice versa. How many times have I stood at cocktail parties listening to gushing enthusiasts attribute to him the work I did while he was still at law school!

How does all of it add up in the pursuit of a career? Problems have ranged from men who felt that since I am not unattractive (I do *not* subscribe to the "sensible" shoes, tight-hair-bun school of thought) and although they really would like to have me in the firm, their wives might misunderstand. Or when I interviewed the Legal Advisor's Office at State Department . . . "We just hired a Negro woman (their first Negro) so we can't use any more."

My tenacity got me past the personnel director to Abram Chayes, then the Legal Advisor, whose wife is also a lawyer. Abe thought I was a great find—a Negro, Jewish, woman lawyer, all for the price of one.

So much for a summing up of the past. As for the future, my son Reuben, looking at a children's book on law which my husband and I had started writing with author Munro Leaf, commented, "Oh, I understand." He muttered as he proceeded through the pages. "That would be really great." And then he added the qualification, "For first or second grade." He turned to us and explained: "You see, when you get to third grade, things get more complicated."

10

RACHEL GOULD

A Satisfying Profession Plus a "Please Forgive Me" Syndrome

Rachel Gould is the pseudonym of a working mother of three young children who is also a child psycologist. She is now in her early thirties and has worked continuously in her profession since her marriage. She analyzes her own motivation for work and the advantages and disadvantages for her family. She sees many of the conflicts and problems of the working mother as coming from our society.

Why one chooses to work, just as whom one decides to marry, are decisions which can never be unraveled because human motivation is too complex and beyond our conscious grasp. In retrospect one likes to think that choices were always infinite, that one had vision into the past and future and deliberately selected the fork in the road that led most directly to one's eventual and final goal. In honesty, however, it takes only a minute amount of introspection to recall the chance play of events out of which irrevocable decisions came. A romance that went awry led directly to a more serious pursuit of one's studies; an admired friend made a choice that had to be emulated. In short, one never is certain to what extent she is the master or the servant of events. However, whether fact or fiction, my decision to have a career seems to have come about as follows.

I was reared in an atmosphere of plenty but awareness of privation was heavily emphasized. In that day, unlike this, it seemed quite possible to change the world for the better. This outlook was accentuated in my family because the notion was inculcated that we children were particularly able, if not gifted. Along with instruction in social injustice, and an evalation of oneself a third ingredient was stressed: the importance of work. Again, in contrast to the present ethos of the young, it was felt in my home that almost any kind of "doing" was preferable to all varieties of "being." Thus one went to work camps when an adolescent to learn about labor and to become familiar with standards of minimal subsistence. The Puritan Ethic assimilated by a Jewish household could only mean one thing: a professional career achieved through an academic route.

It was therefore obvious to me that I would go to college and then to graduate school. I can recall my amazement when friends told me they planned to marry before finishing college. All during my teens the idea of marriage, though very attractive, loomed as a far away possibility. But, as many insulated college girls have found, the long laid-away plans are suddenly challenged by the attractiveness of an intimate relationship with a man, and the weighty social pressure imposed by the norms of the group. I was no exception. It was during my final years at college that my sureness about a professional future became most shaken. I objected to the image associated then with graduate students and career girls. Whenever I mentioned wanting advanced degrees, the implied standard reaction was: "What's the matter with her love life?" I began to have doubts, not only about my abilities with the opposite sex, but my tenacity to sustain the years and difficulties of a graduate education. My visions of becoming, if not a second Freud, then at least in the direct line of his successors, began to crumble. At the end of college I compromised by deciding on a career as a social worker, involving only two more years of study.

Over summer vacations I had worked in neighborhood centers and mental hospitals and had thought that this type of work would be socially useful and personally satisfying. My year in social-work school proved that it wasn't. It taught another lesson: career decisions must be based, at least in the first instance, on an assessment of one's personal abilities and inclinations, not on a sense of obligation. I felt incapable of helping those struggling over problems of survival. What they needed was not middle-class me to listen, but public power to provide. My good will changed into feelings of awkwardness and self-consciousness. My belief in the power of words fled and so did I.

At this point, age 22, I decided to become a child psychologist by getting a doctoral degree in education. This degree was oriented towards practical rather than research work. It would allow me to work in schools, clinics, or privately; part- or full-time. It met a desire for a more academic profession while still satisfying a remaining wish to be of service. By the age of 25 I had completed all the degree requirements with the exception of the thesis and it was then ("finally," thought friends and relations) that I got married. Our first child was born in a year but before the birth of our second, two years follow-ing, I had finished the dissertation and received the coveted degree.

I have worked consistently since my marriage. Due to our frequent changes of residence there have been a series of part-time jobs including diagnostic work, some experi-ence with child therapy, and a smattering of teaching. We now have three children: ages six, four, and two. I work three days a week as a psychologist in a hospital clinic devoted to the identification of pre-school mentally retarded children. I cannot conceive of not working nor have I ever entertained such ideas since the initial career crisis which occurred during my last college years. How-ever there are multiple family problems. Some are caused by our society, some by personal attitudes. There are also personal difficulties.

Since my husband has been totally supportive of my working, indeed would be disappointed were I to consider leaving it, the difficulties I have confronted in continuing my work stem more from two problems in our society rather than any lack of family support. There is first of all the social assumption that enlightened mothers bring up their own children; that they are uniquely and solely qualified to provide their young with the emotional and intellectual sustenance of life. This pernicious doctrine has produced women who feel guilt-ridden each time they leave the peg boards for a public meeting, and whose constant scrutiny of their own behavior has cultivated in them an oversensitivity to the meaning of their children's behavior. The constant watchfulness of self and child, the eagerness to sacrifice oneself while gratifying one's child clearly ends up by harming both. Nonetheless, this is a powerful social ethic and it is hard—at least at first—to turn over the care of one's children to strangers.

The second social problem is that adequate mother substitutes scarcely exist. Although child-care centers are increasing and are widely used by working mothers in other countries, there is something repugnant about placing one's small, vulnerable, middle-class child with scores of others to be watched over by a staff of workers—however professional. The glorification of the family unit has made it uncomfortable for me to place an infant outside its boundaries. Although good arguments can be made for professionalizing the care of the young, one wonders how individuality is fostered when standard environments, standard methods of care, and standard rules prevail. I think that for separateness of self-creativity to flourish, there must be time and space, in the early years at least, for leniency toward, and encouragement of, personal preferences and idiosyncracies. Although some child-care centers and nursery schools have a philosophical belief in individualism, the children are nonetheless confronted with pressures from one another to follow the gang. The lack of solitude and encouragement of socialization may also inadvertantly produce conformity. I therefore have always looked for caretakers to come into our home and they are a rare and disappearing breed. The lack of competent help to care for children has interrupted many a woman's career. It is unfortunate that this line of work is held in such low regard for it surely is more personally satisfying and socially useful than some of the dreary jobs that women would select in preference to it. Perhaps children also would be better off if, for at least part of the day, they were under the tutelage of an objective, dispassionate, kindly adult, who did not see their every move as a personal reflection of her mothering abilities.

Because I have felt neglectful in leaving my children

and because I have had difficulties in fiinding adequate substitutes, I have seen develop a "please forgive me" syndrome. This is probably our most fundamental home problem. There is always the impulse to return from work laden with gifts, an impulse I now inhibit but still feel from time to time. When with the children, I try to make up for time away by being their constant associate. Rules are relaxed. Apologies are made for evenings out. The children therefore object to being left at night. When asked, perhaps in complete innocence and open curiosity, "Why do you go to work, Mommy?" one reels off a well rehearsed panoply of justifications. These "please excuse me" attitudes are obviously harmful to children. An insecure mother makes insecure children, and this leads to demands on the part of the children that mother prove her loyalty and interest. They insist on more and more attention. Jealousies flare. It is this maternal attitude rather than actual time away from the home which seems to me the most harmful effect of combining a career with being a mother. If the mother is completely comfortable about working, her children will be too. If she feels guilty, the children will be upset. It is my experience that guilt is most pronounced when the children are young, ages 18 months to four years. They seem to be most aware then of one's entrances and exists and to be less independent in their interests, less social in their activities. However, if I could easily accept leaving them, I have no doubt they could easily accept my leaving them.

Another family problem arises out of the logistics of one's job. To take children to school with lunches, to nursery school fully equipped with kleenex, to the doctor's, to their lessons, to parties, etc., takes considerable organizing, particularly if one strenuously dislikes arising more than half an hour before any scheduled appointment. These problems, however, are mild compared with the really imposing one of returning from work around 5:00 P.M. confronted with dinner, baths, homework, stories, phone calls—all to be concluded within a few hours. Were children programmed automata it could probably be accomplished but since they have saved up all their tensions, important personal stories, and best of all the endless tales of their altercations with one another until you return, these few hours become very trying. No matter how good the day has been until then, with three children all demanding to be heard simultaneously there is sure to be a conflict—hopefully, but not usually, limited to words—within ten minutes of one's return from work. With the accumulated pressure of a long day at work, mother is not usually at her best and words fly which all wish had been left unsaid. If one can make it through bath time, life usually takes on reasonable proportions again, but there are too many evenings in which explosions, threats, and punishments occur before that hour arrives.

So much for the negative effects of working on the children. There are also personal difficulties involved. The first of these is that there is no time left over for the pursuit of one's own nonfamily nonwork interests. Foresworn are PTA meetings, political activities, pet charities. More important, time is not available for long, lingering talks with friends. Social activities are confined to evenings and therefore involve several couples. Obviously these relationships cannot achieve the intimacy of one-to-one contacts which free time during the day might permit. Although one takes pride in securing the week's groceries on the way home from work while lesser mortals seem to give up many half days to this perfunctory necessity, one nevertheless begins to feel cut off from those things

which are particularly feminine: namely a familiarization
with cultural trends and the refinement of taste. The few
free hours one has in the evening—and they are very few
after the children have been put down, the bills paid,
and the dishes done—are largely spent doing professional
reading, at least when one does not inadvertantly fall
asleep in the process.

A second personal problem lies in the professional area.
Only those with exceptional capacities can be heavily
committed to two time-consuming jobs at one time.
Everyone has their priorities. When faced with whether
to attend a weekend conference (which usually falls
just when one is changing help) or stay at home, my wish
is always to do the latter, though sometimes I reluctantly
pursue the conference. As every professional knows, one
cannot be creative and work by the clock. Insofar as one
wishes to be more than a competent technician, it takes
lots of time: hours to try out new approaches, to read,
to review what one has already done, to talk with others
in related work, to try to forge a small area of expertise.
With the awareness of children clamoring to have you
home—or so one fantasizes—the commitment to work is
of necessity partial. Sometimes one feels like a dilettante,
both in and outside of the home. This problem becomes
even more exaggerated, I should think, when women
begin their professional careers after ten years at home.
To begin at 35 or 40 what others have already been doing
for some time must make it extremely difficult to obtain
any significant stature. The danger then is that work is
what one does because of a self-image and a horror of
home confinement, not because of the inherent fascination
and enjoyment of the work itself.

Given all these personal and family difficulties, the
obvious question is "Why work?" On a personal level,

I could not be happy doing otherwise. It is commonplace today to talk of the accelerating pace of change in all areas of human endeavor. No matter how infinitesimal my role, I want to be a part of these developments. I do not want to drop out of the public world. I suppose every concerned person has his private dream of the political and social power he covets and how he would wield it. In the meantime we passively attend to our laundry and dimly observe the whirlwind around us. Holding a job does not fundamentally change either my fantasies or my passive position, but through working with the public and other professionals I feel a relatedness to those who are trying to make life more rational, more humane, and who are pushing back slightly the curtains of ignorance. To be involved in this is to feel like an adult, and to feel like a more adequate companion to one's husband and friends.

Children also profit, I believe, from the realization that Mommy has more on her mind than their latest squabble with one another. Although not meaning to minimize the importance of children's concerns—it is their total world at the moment they are sharing it with you—they profit from knowing that life goes on beyond the home and school. Although perhaps they cannot assimilate such thoughts when young, as they grow older they hopefully identify with their parents' breadth of interests. In the interim my work helps me—just a bit—to keep perspective on the matters which so concern my children. If I can see their joys and sorrows against a background of the more serious issues with which I am confronted at work, maybe they will be less overwrought by minor matters.

I cannot claim that my children benefit from the fact that I am a psychologist. It is one's early life experience, not assimilated learning, that controls a mother's relationships with her children. I am sometimes able to objectively review a situation I have handled, or mishandled, and approach an understanding of the motivations involved, but this is always after the fact. While the emotions are flying I lead with my feelings.

There are two classes of women I greatly admire. The first is those who, because of their supreme maturity, richness of personality, and contentment, can raise their children, care for their homes and husbands, and lend an air of graciousness to all they touch. Their homes are lively, their children independent and buoyant, their patterns of living always original. Such women—and they are few—probably do more for society than most working mothers. I am not one of them. Were I to stay at home full-time, my interests would sink to the sink; I could preoccupy myself all day with fingerprints, lost mittens, and broken toys. Worse still I would—and do—lose perspective over the minor doings of my children. No relationship can take constant inspection. When the actions and reactions of children are watched too carefully the children become self-conscious and this leads either to an arrogant assertion of self or embarrassed withdrawal. Underlying both forms of behavior is a lack of confidence in spontaneous expression. Thus I feel my work somewhat protects my children from me. Despite wishful thinking and popular mythology, mothers are not an unmixed blessing.

The other group of women I admire are those who are sufficiently self-motivated and clear about their interests, competencies, and how they wish to apportion their time so that they are able to combine being a mother with active volunteer work. Despite the specialization and professionalization of all aspects of modern life, I believe the interested generalist who surveys the scene from some distance, and therefore with perspective, can make enormous contributions to the superior functioning of many institutions. Although considerable controversy exists over whether professionals or lay people should direct organizations, no one would question the contributions that have been made by the nonprofessional. The individual who cares enough to have her idea made part of the social fabric (e.g. by working for or against a piece of legislation) is probably worth a dozen Ph.Ds. I do not have this kind of dedication or persistence; nor have I the strength to work against adversity without any support, be it institutional or monetary. I therefore need a paid job.

The above hopefully explains both why I work and my general view on combining a career with motherhood. The question of whether women should work is much like asking should children eat hot dogs. If they like it, after honest consideration of their family needs and their own talents, they should do it. I see no moral imperative either way. I have come across no evidence which supports the popular notion that children are less secure if their mothers work. The crucial factors which influence children are still unknown, but clearly the mother's working or not working is too gross a variable to be decisive. What undoubtedly count are the subtler interactions between parent and child, not the number of hours spent together. No one would think that the relationship between a hubsand and wife could be measured by hours passed in the same room. Why should it be otherwise for mother and child? Although I do not believe working per se hurts children I see no reason why women should feel obliged to work on the assumption that it is more worthy than staying at home. It does seem to me that with a country so in need of teachers, nurses, and social workers it is a pity that more women do not leave their homes and enter these fields. But with society as it currently exists this cannot be done easily. Therefore much conviction and perserverance are needed. Were I able to order society I would construct living areas with communal laundries and play areas. Women would have no more than two children, and a climate of opinion encouraging women to work would exist. The status of those interested in caring for the young would be raised. Given the limits of our society, women must make their choices and their sacrifices. On one matter, however, I feel strongly. It is an error to refrain from a much desired professional life because of a burdensome conscience which dictates that one must give full-time care to the children. The likely result—and who has not seen this pattern repeated time and again—is that after a valiant effort and a few happy years there is a headlong plunge into ennui and depression. We are people first and mothers second. We cannot deny an important area of our personalities without dire results. When duty and desire become bifurcated one acts either on impulse or out of obligation. These are bad alternatives, and a dilemma one frequently observes in women. If one chooses to work, it should be done without remorse and if one elects to stay home, it should be pleasurable and fulfilling.

11

CAROLINE PERRY

Mother's Going Back to School Is Hard on All of Us

Caroline Perry is the pseudonym of a part-time graduate student, part-time writer, and full-time mother and wife. She is in her late thirties and has done some free-lance writing before and during her present study. She graduated from college fifteen years ago and now has six children ranging from preschool to teenagers. She is an example of the older woman who returns to study in preparation for a second career. She finds the transition from full-time motherhood to a combination of work and family very difficult, but necessary for her well-being.

I must admit that I am in constant emotional conflict over the different claims of my children and my work. When I calmly try to analyze why I feel this way and how I got into this situation, I can see several emerging patterns in my past life and development. From my earliest childhood I wanted to marry, have many, many babies, *and* do great things in the world. I never could give up one ambition for the other. I was eager to live, to love, to achieve, and to be fruitful in every possible womanly way.

I have never had any conscious jealousy of boys because (1) they could not wear lipstick, curls, pretty clothes, or have babies and (2) it never occurred to me that boys would have opportunities denied to me. I was never even a tomboy. From six on I was always madly in love with someone, calculating cosmetics, courtship and marriage while trying to decide whether I really wanted to be the first lady president. I was as eager to learn to sew as I was to excel in studies and sports. My father and mother encouraged me in all directions. Perhaps as the eldest daughter in a two-child family with no boys, I never mentally split the male and female role into opposite poles, or even imagined that I should accept a secondary role in achievement. My parents encouraged me to be both very feminine *and* very educated and successful. They thought I should establish a career (maybe as a doctor) before I married, so I could be completely independent and self-sufficient.

Yet curiously enough, at the same time I was getting career encouragement, I was also taught (and accepted) that within marriage the patriarchial model was normal and right. Husbands were to be dominant. It was a terrible thing for women to be more aggressive than their husbands. Thus, it was very suspicious if a woman worked after marriage, since social life with her husband and maternal duties should take all of a woman's time. Careers and work competence were for before marriage and in case of emergencies afterward. Like many another American girl, I was encouraged to achieve and work until marriage—but marriage would suddenly end it all. My parents never faced the split between their ambitions for me as a person and other contradictory assumptions about the correct behavior of a wife and mother. Neither did I.

Much of my other formative experience in middle class culture was also encouraging to feminine ambition. Growing up on the East Coast in the '40s and '50s, going to a girls' prep school and women's college, whose reputations depended on the achievement of their graduates, I was certainly pushed to achieve. Get those grades, get into an ivy league school, get into graduate school, get to the top and make us proud. At the same time, friends and family were equally insistent that I remain feminine and popular, and marry well. I thoroughly agreed with both goals and studied frantically and dated frantically.

At that pace I came quickly to the impasse that the culture sneaks into the system to comfound ambitious young women who want the best of both worlds. After so many years of dating and so many years of intense academic specialization, I was biologically, socially, and emotionally ready at 21 to get married. The perfect mate had appeared on the scene and my desires for love, home, and family were overwhelming. They did not extinguish the desires for intellectual life and achievement which my husband-to-be shared. Both of us wanted to be married, have children, and continue studying. But economically and socially this was impossible.

The hard facts of life were inexorable. My husband had to go through years more of schooling and we could never afford the double tuition and household help necessary for both of us to study. We could just barely survive on the G.I. bill's provisions. All of my husband's energy would be used up in studying and supporting me and the children we both wanted right away. I was forced to the terrible conclusion that for me in my circumstances it was children or career. Why was this so final?

In the city in which my husband was enduring the

ordeal of graduate study there were no graduate schools which accepted beginning students part-time. Nor were there scholarships and fellowships for part-time students. Girls could only get into graduate school if they could give as much time to it as a single man. Any family provisions for housing, etc. were directed to the married male graduate student. There were absolutely no child-care facilities available which could free a young mother for study or work. The only possible child-care arrangements were individual, private, and expensive. I myself made money babysitting other people's children in our apartment, a practice called "parking" children. I had no intention of "parking" my child or my children with anyone less qualified than myself. In most arrangements it was impossible to control the quality of care or to know the relationship of the "parked" child and the children in the home. Very few other mothers came up to my standards of care, nor could I see enduring the emotional wear and tear of taking the children from home and depositing them in another home. In our isolated, penny-pinching situation far from our families we had to provide all the security for our children. With a husband burdened to the breaking point, I had to be even more the main provider of a stable, secure environment. Moreover, no one but a mother would be willing to work in such poor, crowded quarters with such an arduous routine. Not many people with good qualifications for child care were available for domestic work in a three room slum apartment; nor could I have possibly afforded any such person.

In those early struggling years of marriage I was forced to choose between my two ambitions for a big family and a big career. I had to devise a new plan to cope with the harsh realities of American culture. I would speedily

have my children (all six that I desired), and then after
my husband had finished school and my children had
entered school, I would go back to school and gradually
enter the professional world. In the meantime I would
master the domestic world of home and family and
educate myself with all the reading I had not had a
chance to do in college. This plan worked relatively well
while we lived in a graduate school community. I could
discuss the high-level reading I did with others and get
new stimulating ideas. Since we live in a poor, struggling
student ghetto my domestic work also had meaning. My
work was obviously necessary for survival and was often
shared with other young families. We helped one another
and gave support and care with what we had. Even so,
the lack of time for study still caused me as much suffering as the hard work and worry of bearing and rearing
many small children with little money. Yet because of
the purposefulness of the work and the intellectual and
social community, I felt that I was maturing and growing.
While I envied my husband his chance for graduate study,
my own life seemed even more significant and real.

After we moved from our friendly, intellectual slum,
things were different. My husband was through school
and working far away in the city. I was stuck in a house in
a middle-class suburb where everyone was relatively self-
sufficient. In this setting, without a specialized intellectual
community, my private reading and study seemed pointless. Domestic life also was more boring without the companionship of other young mothers or the feeling of serving
more than just my own family. With more money many
of the old tasks became pointless. Why sew baby overalls
to save a dollar when a dollar more or less makes no
difference? For me, the less arduous domestic life was, the
more boring. Without enough challenge or community or

intellectual stimulation, I felt half alive and miserable. Soon I was desperate with boredom and depression.

The time had come to reassess my plans. I could no longer wait as long as I had thought I could; I could not sacrifice one part of me to the other. In my suburban circumstances the price had become too high. After a decade of exclusive domesticity I had to make a change to a new way of life. Since I could not yet afford the time or money for graduate school I made a decision to begin some other work beyond the home and family. I had three more babies after this basic decision, but from that point on, my life took on a new and different dimension. I would now attempt to combine nondomestic work and child rearing. Essentially I am still in this time of transition from full-time motherhood to motherhood combined with a career. For me this has to be a slow process.

After struggling through some writing projects which finally brought in some funds, I enrolled in graduate school. I am now midway to getting a graduate degree, with six children aged thirteen to three. Frankly, I find the transition to a professional role extremely difficult. First of all, there is the inner emotional problem. I do feel badly leaving my two little children who are not yet in school. My big children hardly know I do any outside work since they are at school when I am at school and I am home when they arrive.

But the two little ones, three and four, would rather have me at home. They even say frequently "Don't work" and "Stay with us." They are jealous of my other interests and often cry when I leave them or shout when I must study. When I first come home they are often extremely demanding and obstreperous. I am rarely away at school or working in my study for more than five or six hours, and I give them attention all the rest of the time, yet still they are disturbed by many of my departures. Having once been a full-time mother I know that in my case my small children's day goes better with me as sole caretaker. *I* am a hundred times happier with a portion of the day for intellectual work, but I am not sure that my children are better off.

I am sure that my children are not being seriously harmed, but if I could make more sacrifices and stay home I think they would be happier and calmer. Since I can no longer make these sacrifices without deep depression, I comfort myself by remembering the occasional breakdowns in the old regime from my fatigue and resentments. I can see also that having substitute care may toughen my rather spoiled children and make them more flexible. But it also makes their lives more strained. So I worry about working and find that some departures exhaust me more than the work I do for the rest of the day.

Another difficulty, of course, comes with the problems involved in having a substitute caretaker. This is an insoluble problem as far as I can see. Unattractive helpers make it harder to see mommy go, and attractive, permissive help sets up occasional conflicts in the child over his allegiance. Helpers are invariably more strict or more permissive than parents. Sometimes the difference in techniques can be dangerous, with bribery one problem and threats another. If one is a good mother, one can always do better than the best help available. For that matter, it is often a long, lucky process to find a helper at all.

The huge amount of money necessary to hire good help is one problem, but not the only one to be faced. The complicated kind of permissive child rearing desired by educated American parents requires intelligence, judgment, and a delicate use of authority. Few hired helpers can be given enough authority to cope with independent, intelligent older children. They need the firm hand and authority of a parent to control them. I have found that as hard as it is to leave my small children with a substitute, it is even harder to leave my older boys when they are home. They need my wisest and firmest supervision. Since they are so independent they need parents even more when they are home. I worry about these more subtle demands of my older children. At this point I think that I may never take a full-time job unless I can be home when they come home (or don't come home).

Fortunately, at the present moment I have adequate help for the first time since I began a double career. I have a live-in helper who is young but not a teen-ager. She comes from the British Isles, and is more like a young relative from overseas than a hired helper; her personality and approaches to child rearing are consistent with mine. She also provides the extra margin of help so necessary to a mother going out of the home. My baby-sitters left when I came home, leaving me with all the cooking, cleaning, and child care for the rest of the day. Now I have enough help so I can be more leisurely and attentive to the children. The house is less cluttered and dirty, and I am not always exhausted. Of course, such a financial drain is something that few other families can afford. I can pay the price because, luckily, I can earn money as well as go to school. Other families would have to have a very rich husband, fewer children, and/or borrow money.

Another nonfinancial price to be paid in a double career is the drastic stripping of leisure from one's life. Going to graduate school and having a big family takes every available minute of the day. There is rarely time for recreation of any kind. Even if one does take a night off to look at TV or go to a movie, there is the nagging guilt about work that is not yet done. Social life also becomes a luxury since time with the children is a primary necessity. Worry over leaving the children for work makes the rest of the time extremely child centered.

Yet we have also found that it is very unhealthy for children to live in a home without access to an adult world into which they can grow. They need to see parents having a stimulating, adult social life. This is all the more necessary when they cannot comprehend the rewards of intellectual life nor in any way participate in our study and work. We have resorted to having company and house guests frequently instead of going out. We have learned that great care needs to be taken that home and family are not impoverished in the interests of parental achievement. Asceticism has to be curbed in order to avoid the collapse of the parents and the shortchanging of the children. They need a joyful richness in family life as well as the necessities. Two parents alone cannot give children a sense of an adult community.

We have found that the increased number of adults in their lives is one good thing in favor of having help in the home. If the adult helpers also provide more adult support for the mother and father, it is an added asset. In our lively, hectic family situation it is wonderful to have another adult to add to the adult team. When I worry most about working I remember the better family organization we have now compared to the minimum for survival we had before.

My worries are also quelled by the necessities which ease decision-making. Psychologically, I know that it is necessary for me to go out of the home because I can barely endure life without some continuously demanding intellectual work. Without sustained intellectual stimulation, I literally go to pieces. Financially it is also necessary that I make my contribution to the family. Although the cost of help is terrible (and it is an unfair law that does not allow this as a tax exemption) we still make needed money from my working. With the prospect of at least three continuously in college for some ten years, we will need my income no matter how small it might be. My hope is that as the children grow older and are all in school the conflicts and worries of this transitional time will be lessened. My part-time and maybe full-time work will be established as a fixture in family life in all of our minds, so that conflicts will disappear.

Also I hope that my husband will become even more totally reconciled as this time of difficult transition passes. While he has helped me and encouraged me with many sacrifices of time there has been a lingering, almost unconscious, resistance. His burdens of work are so heavy that any added complication of life seems threatening. Also there seems to be some irrational fear of having an independent wife capable of a high-level career. I think that in my husband's anxious moments he is a little jealous of my outside interests and is afraid that I might find professional life more engrossing than life as wife and mother. I am offended by this suspicion since to me it is obvious that no outside work can satisfy my desires for a happy family life. In a real showdown I will always put my husband and children first.

Then again, in our competitive culture husband and working wife have to make strong efforts not to be competing. Undoubtedly, the fear of being overshadowed by one's mate is more of a male problem than a female one. Yet both partners must resist the comparisons of their "friends" and work to turn all efforts into joint family projects. The wife's work is one more area in which the

delicate balance of individuality and the good of the
family have to be adjusted. Unfortunately, even the best
of men, such as my exemplary husband, who can rationally
and actively support their wife's equality and work, can
still harbor a remnant of their lifetime conditioning in
male prerogatives. They have to struggle, much like the
reformed white Southerner, to rid themselves of preju-
diced and inconsistent assumptions.

I have suffered most when caught in the double bind
presented by an enlightened husband in transition. Yes,
work and bring in money, but also be an absolutely perfect wife and mother. A husband who finds himself under
pressure from his wife's new activities can be more hyper-
critical than anyone. While criticism from the neighbors
may hurt, it can never be as difficult to cope with as that
of a beloved mate. Only a continual reappraisal and
purification of motive, along with perfect self-discipline,
gets a wife through the bad times. In marriage you must
take the other with you when you grow and change, so
growing and changing in one way means you have to grow
in love too. It's an effort but ultimately seems worthwhile.
I am happier than I have ever been despite conflicts and
complexities.

I am raising my sons and daughters for what I hope is
a newly emerging culture. I give them as best I can strong
male and female physical sexual identities, but stress
equal dignity and the need for men and women to be both
tender and achieving. Both work and family care are
important human capabilities. The joy of womanhood,
I tell them, is being able to have babies and boys are
physically stronger in order to protect the weak (including
babies). Personalities and work roles are not sex typed
but depend on talent, interest, and capacity. In other
words, I want my children to be healed of my inner con-

traditions. I want them to be free to make choices I could not make without grief and not to be forced into other decisions. If society can change, then both my sons and daughters can live fuller lives. In a more ideal society, my painful conflicts and struggles may seem quaint. What only a few of my generation can struggle to do today, many more may freely do tomorrow.

I understand that very few will want all that I have wanted. Not many will desire the challenge and delights of many children as well as the ecstasy of hard intellectual tasks. I do not scorn those more capable than myself of leisure, cultural pursuits, and volunteer community work. But society should ease up on the women who above all desire intense family life and intense absorbing work. We need more scholarships, more flexible work requirements, more trained domestic help, and revised expectations from the world. We shouldn't be penalized for being ambitiously female as well as intellectually ambitious. Some of my conflicts over a double role may be unavoidable, but part of freedom is the freedom to choose which conflicts to bear.

12

ANNE WILLIAMS

I Find Working
Is a Relief;
I Love My Work

Anne Williams is the pseudonym of a widowed black mother of five grown children. Over the years she has held many different jobs, many in domestic and custodial work. Now she is a teacher's aide in the public school of a large city ghetto. In the summer and through the year she teaches in a church school. She has found work both a financial necessity and a form of self-fulfillment.

Q: [1] How did you come to be a working mother?

A: In 1951 I moved here with my husband and five children. In 1953 it came to the point where we separated because he didn't have a good job and things weren't

[1] This account of the experience of combining work and child rearing was written from a personal interview. Both the interviews and the essays in this book derived from the questionnaire which appears in the Appendix.

going too well. There were arguments and arguments so we went to court and separated.

Q: Did it have anything to do with the welfare system, where men desert their families to get welfare assistance?

A: No, he didn't desert the family for that reason. It was just one of those things. He didn't have a good job. Sometimes if you're very weak and meet up with the wrong people they're going to keep you in your same category. You just don't do anything. He was a weak person although he had good skills.

Q: It must have been a difficult time.

A: True. It is very hard to have a houseful of children. I had five children. I had to be in the house at all times being responsible for everything. You know you have a husband but he's not—I don't know what's on his mind, but anyway he doesn't show interest. He doesn't see that he's got to help or get a good job or just stick together and pull it out. It gets to the point a woman gets disgusted and lots of women leave the children; but I said, "Well, I'll never leave mine."

Q: How old were they?

A: Well the oldest was nine when we separated. But then I came in contact with the church through the children. So I've stuck with the church and the church has lots of things to offer the children, like the friendly times we have here at the church school. I was able to manage. You look around and you say, "Here I am with a houseful of kids, no money, no job, with a husband that's not helping." What could I do? We went to court. At that time we were seeing the welfare and a couple of times he would come home and say I need some money to do something and I'll give you the money back tomorrow. He did that twice and took the money from the children where I didn't have money to buy food. I decided then it must stop. This has to be stopped. So I called the investigator and she asked me to get him over to the center. I managed to get him over there because I felt like it wasn't right for them to send money. And he wasn't living there. And he would take the money and the children were hungry. That way we were able to get a separation. After I did it, I was frightened. I think God is good because things went along very well after.

Q: Did you ever work before that?

A: Yes, I was working. I always worked because I was working at Penn station during the war.

Q: Tell me about when you were a little girl, and your family. Did they think women should work? Where did you grow up?

A: I grew up in North Carolina, Kingston, North Carolina. In our family everybody had to work. We all had duties to do.

Q: How many were there?

A: There were six of us. We all had certain duties. I was the only girl though. I had to do all the laundry, the washing.

Q: Did your mother work?

A: She more or less worked. My father took in a lot of working hands. He had a big farm and we more or less worked around the house taking care of them, feeding, preparing food for all those people. I imagine you can picture that.

Q: Yes.

A: So that was really a steady job.

Q: You mean her job was a steady job? A farm wife is a real occupation?

A: Being a farm wife is quite a duty. But I left all of that and came to the city.

Q: How old were you when you left home?

A: I went out on my own very young. I was 16. I had a stepmother and I didn't really like her. She wasn't very nice to us. Usually when you find your home life not so enjoyable or comfortable you look for other things.

Q: What about your schooling? Did you have the feeling that you should be getting schooling? Or did you not think about that at the time?

A: After I left home I went to school in the evening, and I worked during the day part-time. I was working for a lawyer and I wanted to go to school so bad, but I never did get a chance to finish my education because I had to work and support myself.

Q: It's a drain.

A: It really is. When I look around now and see the kids who have it so good! Everything is just handed to them. I think about myself when I was growing up.

Q: Did you work for this lawyer in North Carolina after you left home?

A: Yes. I worked for him after I left home. They were very kind to me, just like I was part of the family.

Q: Did you work in the family?

A: Yes I did, I worked in the family. I helped them with their little boy and I did the shopping. She did all the cooking but I was just there more or less to help her.

Q: Mother's helper?

A: Yes, mother's helper. After I left them I was working for other people in Kingston, North Carolina and there I went to school. After I left there I met my husband when I was young. Had I not been so young I would have waited a little while. So I left Kingston and came to the city where my family really did grow.

Q: Had you any children before you came up here?

A: Only one. The oldest son was born in North Carolina, all the rest were born here.

Q: When you came here, did you get a job right away?

A: Yes, I did. This is when I began working at the USO; there were a lot of soldiers at that time. We kept the USO in order for the soldiers and it was a very interesting job.

Q: What did you do with your children when you went to work?

A: I could always get a babysitter. The neighbors were around and they were always willing to take care of the children.

Q: Did you find that it was financially still worthwhile, if you paid them?

A: It more or less took what I earned to pay, but just getting out of the house into a different atmosphere made you feel better. When you come out to work and go back, you know you are going back to more work but it was rewarding because it would give you a different feeling. You're not doing the same thing over and over again. At night I would go in and prepare supper and prepare the clothes that they would use the next day, and take food to this lady.

Q: For the children?

A: This is why she didn't charge me as much, because I would take their food and have it all prepared so she could just warm it and feed it to them. It was really hard work because it would be late at night when I got to bed, but I was determined. This went on and on until things weren't getting any better.

Q: You were determined to have money and to have an income so that your children wouldn't be—

A: Lacking for different things.

Q: Yes.

A: Because during those years things weren't really as well as they are now. We didn't make that much money, but still and all its up to the person. If he had been used to certain things all of his life and if it is really in his mind that he is going to do good regardless of how hard things are I think he can make it. But it has to be planted there, he'd have to be determined. You can't give up. You can't give up hope.

Q: Yes. Did you like this lady who took care of your children? Did you think that she did well by the children?

A: I liked this lady very well because she had grand-children of her own and I knew her for a long time. I felt very safe. I felt that she took care of the children.

Q: The way you would do it if you were there?

A: Yes. After I moved out of that neighborhood I didn't work any more. My kids were getting to come fast. I didn't work any more until after my daughter was out of junior high school.

Q: About how many years did you stay home?

A: I think that must have been about five or six years.

Q: You felt that you couldn't take more than two to this place?

A: Right. Because she had other children too. This is why I felt that she would do well, because she had other mothers' children. I felt like we all would see how she did. Since we would all look and watch the children, the mothers proved that we cared. We all carried food to make sure that there was no mistaking about having the children fed properly.

Q: Could she take them out at all? That's the difficult thing in the city, not being able to get out with the children.

A: Yes, at that time we were able to. We lived near a park, only a half a block from the park and she had an older daughter that would help her out with the children in the park and help her back. It didn't go on too long because it is a frightening thing when you know that they're out on the street and so many things could happen.

Q: Would they cry when you left them?

A: No, they didn't because this lady was living in the same building we were living in and they knew her. More or less the children liked seeing their friends. She was very good with them because you can always tell when a child is not treated well—they don't want to go back. We watched all those things. I wouldn't say they loved it too much but they knew that this was something their mother was doing every day, leaving them. I'm sure they didn't quite understand why it had to be. When I moved here in this area I didn't work. I stayed in the house.

Q: Do you think that your husband resented your work at the beginning? Was he happier when you stayed home?

A: I never thought of it because he didn't ever say anything. He knew why I was working, because he wasn't making that much money.

Q: Well, did he resent it when you stayed home then, and didn't have money?

A: No, he didn't say anything one way or another. I mean he didn't say anything.

Q: It seemed utterly indifferent to him.

A: That's true. Only when we went to court and we were speaking about these things he said, "This woman didn't have to work." The judge said to him, "Well, how could she work with all these children and take care of them?" Maybe it was in his mind but he never did express whether he liked it or not.

Q: But you felt that by that remark that he showed that he resented it a bit?

A: Yes. I did think about it after he had said that. But, on the other hand, he never did grudge me to say that you should get a job and help. That was just my idea.

Q: You felt that that was the way one ought to do it?

A: Yes. That was the way I wanted to do it. I don't know whether this had anything to do with the separation.

Q: Did you feel that your working was more of a financial necessity or more of a need to do different things and get out of the house?

A: To me at the time of the children I did it so that I could have money to do more things for them. So I could buy them clothing, because sometimes after the rent was paid, and the food, there was never anything left to buy any clothing, to buy them a pair of shoes, a pair of boots, a little dress or something. Then after a while when they got bigger I discovered it was nice to be out among people and you're meeting people. Sometimes you look at yourself and say I am so bad off and then you get out and see others are worse than you. I find working is a relief after a while. It is a relief. It's much better than staying in the house and doing the same things over and over. I don't think I could stay in the house now. I love my work now being a teacher's aide in the school and teaching in the church school.

Q: When you stayed home and were having children at that time, did you have any feeling that you wanted to stop having so many children? Did you use birth control to plan in-between, or was it just that you wanted a big family and this is the way it turned out?

A: To tell the truth I don't know. As the years go by I guess I can see that it was the environment that I was in. We weren't really educated to these things as the mothers are now. I'm sure it was going on—family planning, but sometimes you're in the wrong neighborhood and without the right contacts or the right friends to help you to think. I guess I was all tied up in my own life, my home life wasn't happy. A wife can get to the point that she just gets into a rut and she doesn't meet people. I really wasn't associated with any church. I was living in a Jewish neighborhood. We didn't have a church. I have discovered that this is where you get a lot of contacts with the right things, because in church people get up and make announcements about different things. I find it very rewarding being out in public, this is how you learn how to think.

Q: You didn't have any religious feeling against birth control?

A: I liked children. I always liked children. I always said that if I could have ten pregnancies I would have them. I never did like the idea of doing anything to prevent having them. After a while, you say you can't take care of all of these children if you bring them into the world. I felt this with the last pregnancy with my daughter. "Now after this I can't go on." I think that if my home life had been different I would have felt differently. So, after my daughter I really didn't get pregnant any more because we separated. But I enjoyed my children so much as they began to grow.

Q: So you felt that while it was hard being home, it served a purpose at that time. You couldn't have done as well going out to work?

A: Right, after the kids began to grow I was there to answer their needs and calls. I know that just about a month ago, my children and I were speaking about what a hard time I had when they were growing up and I said I think about that very dearly now. I couldn't give you this and I couldn't give you that. My oldest one said to me, "Ma, you shouldn't even say that because you were there, you gave us love." That means more to me than anything in the world. You look around at other families that had more to offer but there was no love there. He also said, "We didn't have a father and I've seen lots of things I wished I hadn't seen. But it brought us closer to you."

Q: How old are they now?

A: They are 24, 19, 20, 22, and 25.

Q: When did you start back to work then?

A: When my daughter was in her last year of junior high school. And when they were small I was working. Every time I had a baby I would find some place to work, that's when I should have been home at the time, but I found the time to work.

Q: Then you stopped?

A: Yes, I stopped after a while. First, I worked at a hotel as a housekeeper, but it was always part-time jobs and I was always lucky to find someone right in my building to keep the kids. When I moved here, in this area in this development, I didn't have any close friends and I couldn't. This is when I had to stop, because before I was always lucky to find some lady in the building who could look after the children, who liked children, someone whom I liked and we were close and I respected her. I think that's what kept me going, having children and the babies and having to stay at home—I don't think I could have took it. Getting out is what I think really kept me going through the years.

Q: Once your daughter went to junior high and all the bigger boys were grown you felt that you could work again. Do you think your example of working did anything for them?

A: My oldest son, when he finished high school he tried a number of jobs—as a salesman, in a hospital—and then he was a model for *Ebony* magazine. He tried all types of things. Then he was drafted. Now he's working as a private nurse. He works way out in Long Island in private duty. I guess so, because he discovered that he did have to work.

Q: But they did finish school?

A: Yes, he did finish high school. And the second boy, he's been in school most of the time, so he's a second lieutenant and will soon be a first lieutenant within two more weeks. He had two years of college and he's finishing the rest of his education in the service. And the third boy he's got six months to finish high school. I think the three younger ones got caught up in the thing that's happening all over the world. Because Benjie the third boy is a very smart boy. In fact all of the children were very smart when it comes to their books. But I think the three young ones are weak. My daughter finished high school, so all finished but one. The fourth boy found the going rough, going with the wrong crowds, so I just caught a hold of him and put him in a training school so he finished his education there. I felt it was best to do that instead of just going on. This neighborhood, I would say, is a snake pit. This is what it is. Because the very best child if he is not strong will get swallowed up by a snake. This is what we call it. Because there is always a vulture out there ready to grab you. They pick on the kids that they know that they can conquer—the little good ones who they feel have money. My son was going on nine and a man used to come around the block at the candy stores and give the kids little cigarettes to smoke and so on. But he told me all about it.

Q: Well, without a father too. Did your husband take an interest in the boys at all?

A: My husband got to the place where he was drinking— he turned to drink—and he's dead now. He died.

Q: So he couldn't help at all.

A: No, there's no help at all. The most help that I got was from the ministers of the church.

Q: Was there any kind of day care or other public help at all?

A: Let's see, what's happened through the years? I had sent my boys away to Friend Town, the camp, but this one particular summer the school had gotten my boy this job. The Youth Corps had begun to work with all the kids in this area so he wanted to work and I thought it was good, because he never had any money and I thought it was good because they like to have some money and this was the way to get it. But while he was working he was easy, and he was making money, and they were standing on the corner—so this is just how it all began. It was a hopeless feeling. It got to the point I felt like it was going to just keep on going. So we managed to get him away in a training school. That was the only way we could save him.

Q: Yes.

A: So it didn't come out exactly like I wished all the way but it could have been much worse.

13

PATRICIA JORDAN

Deliver Me from Disorganization and the Tax Man

Patricia Jordan is in her late thirties and has two small children. Before her marriage she was a television producer and director. She has now returned to free-lance work in television and relates why out-to-work is more satisfying to her than stay-at-home work. She also speaks of the financial dilemma that the tax laws impose on the mother who works.

One thing must be made clear at the start: there is no such thing as a *non*working mother. There are paid, employed, go-off-to-a-job-in-the-morning mothers. There are unpaid but fully employed take-care-of-the-children-husband-house-and-all-the-other-things mothers. The differences between the two groups are small, and to my way of thinking have mainly to do with time. The quality of time devoted to the various parts of their lives, not the quantity, makes for the greatest difference. The out-to-worker will enjoy fully her children's tales between home-coming and bedtime, and hand out store-bought cookies. The stay-home-worker may listen with only half an ear to the children's all-day chatter, and enjoy fully having them help her bake.

Fragmentation characterizes the time of the stay-at-home mother. She must be able to do three things at once, and change roles many times a day.

Organization had better characterize the time of the out-to-worker. She has to know within a fairly rigid frame what she and the rest of the family will be doing, not tomorrow, but a week from now. And she must have planned for most contingencies. Before my marriage, I produced and directed public affairs television programs for NBC's New York station. I had an apartment in the city, spent weekends with my parents in the country, worked extremely hard, and earned—for a woman—a great deal of money. And I enjoyed all of it. Frank Jordan, the man I was to marry, lived very much the same sort of life, working in television news for NBC . . . but in Chicago. Clearly, commuting was out. When we married, I quit, moved to Chicago, and settled down to nest-building. Two children just a year apart left me the time and inclination to go back to work only for a few weeks during the 1960 Republican and Democratic conventions.

We were transferred back to New York early in 1963. Our first house and two toddlers were a full-time job for a year and a half. In the summer of 1964, I called the Directors' Guild to ask for part-time work. (I suppose it is indicative of being basically work-oriented that I had faithfully paid my union dues during those nonworking years.) Since it was again an election year, my husband would be home very little until mid-November; since the children were now three and two and got along very well together, it seemed a good time to try it.

Part-time work in television production differs from part-time work, say, in a store. Working in a store usually implies a few hours a day several days a week, every week. In television, part-time means being hired for a specific show, and for the three weeks or so during which the show is rehearsed, taped, and edited, production people have to be available for any number of hours a day, seven days a week. When the program is finished, free-lance production people either move on to another job, or, in my case, go home to catch up on the family, the laundry, the garden. It is very satisfactory for me to know that no one style of living is going to go on for too long at a stretch. It is possible simply to put off for three weeks washing the windows, and easier than trying to sandwich such a chore into a weekend that should be relaxation between the Friday and Monday of a regular job. It is also possible, if you're not too enthusiastic about housework, to use this sort of job situation as a carrot in front of the donkey: "I vow I'll clean those bureau drawers before I take another job."

I did not go back to work as a producer or director, for several reasons. For one think, my experience was in the sorts of programs usually done by network staff employees, not free-lancers. For another, it had been several years since I had worked in New York, I had not been that well known as a director, and many of the people I had known in the industry—television jobs frequently come through contacts—were no longer in positions where I could ask them for jobs. Either they had gone to the West Coast, along with most productions, or they had got to be famous, or vice-presidents, and it would have been presuming on old friendships to have asked for work. There is another reason, too. Producers and directors have twenty-four-hour-a-day jobs. Rarely can they turn off during the train ride home and arrive at the door ready to pay full attention to the family. Altogether, it seemed to me too demanding a career for a woman who enjoys her husband and family. So, with a substantial cut in money *and* responsibility, I arrived at a workable compromise, and went back to work as an assistant to the producer-director. This job can mean almost anything, depending on the network's definition of the job, the demands and competence of the producer-director, and on the competence and adaptability of the assistant. In a way, and I must admit I never thought of this before, it is a little like being a wife (running a house). Most wives are not responsible for the major decisions in their homes—how to make a living, where a career is leading, whether to change jobs—although they participate in the decision-making process. In addition to contributing as much as she can to these basic decisions and choices of goals, the wife is responsible for: as much comfort as she can give her husband and family, a pleasant atmosphere, and all the details. In very much the same way the production assistant is not responsible for the overall success of a program, but can contribute to it by seeing to all the details, making it easy for the creative producer to concentrate on basics. Although the situations are somewhat analagous, there is one major difference between home and television: at the studio one is dealing with adults, people whose talents and interests are similar to one's own. In contrast, at home, the conversation of even the most delightful child palls sooner or later.

After doing one "special" at CBS, and several religious dramas at ABC, I was hired as production assistant on Leonard Bernstein's "Young People's Concerts" to work for Roger Englander. This was very exciting. I had admired Roger's work for a long time, and was eager to watch him at it. And the opportunity to work with Bernstein and the New York Philharmonic was wonderful. There are four concerts during a television season, spaced so that my schedule worked out to three weeks on, two weeks off, three weeks on, a month off—a total of twelve weeks' work over a period of five months.

That, not too briefly, is what I have been doing as a paid working wife and mother. But working is the adjective—or adjectival gerund if you will—and wife and mother are the nouns. Given that the nouns are of prime importance, why do I insist on the modifier? Why do I work? How do I arrange my life with husband, children, and social and community obligations in order to satisfy them all and do my job? Is it worth it?

Why do I work? Because I enjoy it. Having learned television production from the bottom up, I really like exercising and extending that knowledge. I work for my own personal satisfaction. And although this sort of decision—whether to work for pay or not—has to be a personal decision for every woman, there are, I think, certain prerequisites common to all of us who decide to take on a paid job away from the house: interest, enthusiasm, a real desire to do the job you know, and a need—whether it be pure personal satisfaction or the necessity in your own mind to be someone other than Jimmy's mother. These are the only things that will get you up, dressed, coiffed, made up; the kids up, dressed, fed, school-lunched; your husband fed and cosseted if need be—mine doesn't thank heaven, he wakes up cheery—and you out of the house in time for work with grocery lists and instructions left for that mythical mother's helper we call Nice Nellie around our house. Only if you have all these attitudes plus a fine sense of priorities should you go out to work.

Never go out to work because you think you can use the money. That is the one piece of unqualified advice I shall offer. Unless you already have Auntie living with you, and she's marvelous with the children, and very eager to run the house, you probably can't afford it. For one thing, competent household help comes very high. For another, the clothes suitable for Matronly Suburban Activities—blue jeans and grubby sneakers—will not do for work. Add in lunches (never mind if you're always on a diet, the coffee wagon comes around at 20 cents a throw for an apple) and commuting costs. And the last depressing straw: your shoe bill will probably treble. It might even be higher than the shoe bill for the kids!

Let us assume then, that you want to go to work, that you can find help at a price which is less than your own salary, and that you find a job you want to take. You are still at a financial disadvantage. Two financial disadvantages, as a matter of fact. First off, I know of no companies who will consider a husband and wife's combined income when making withholding tax deductions. What that means is that even if you take "0" deductions on that W-2 withholding form, the company or the government or whoever, is going to withhold only the maximum percentage against *your* salary . . . not the maximum percentage of your salary combined with your husband's. You make, say, $100 a week. As a for instance, let's suppose your husband makes $1,000 a week. If you put down "0" deductions on your tax information form with your company, they will take out the largest tax they can withhold, but it will be against an annual income of $5,200 rather than against a combined annual income of $57,200. This is an extreme example, but you can see how April 15th will be a shocker when you go (back) to work.

Financial disadvantage number two is one of my large gripes. Unless you are a model, your clothes, cosmetics, shoes, and so on, are not a deductible business expense.

Not many of us are models. The salary of the doctor's secretary, however, who minds the store while he is out making calls, *is*, for him, deductible as a business expense. And, if your husband does part of his work at home, as mine does, so is a percentage of the light, water, gas, telephone, repair, and depreciation on your house. Not so for the woman who goes out to work. Henrietta Housekeeper, who minds the store when we are out working, is not deductible from any point of view unless you are a widow, or head of household. And there is financial disadvantage number two—with a vengeance. What it comes down to is that your going out to work is liable to boost your family income into a higher tax bracket and yet not yield much in the way of added cash money to spend. In spite of these things, there is an ever-increasing number of women who simply must "do their thing." More power to them, I say.

In my case, going to work is selfishly based. I truly enjoy the turmoil of television more than full-time housekeeping and motherhood. I love reading to the kids, talking with them, digging in the garden with them, popping corn, and acting silly. I do not enjoy supervising poster paint, washing windows, settling squabbles, mucking around in papier maché or thinking up Things to Do. So I come home from work eagerly, knowing I can look forward to an enthusiastic greeting. They are fresh from their baths, in their pajamas, ready for stories, ready to exchange the days' adventures. They are pleased to see the best of me—not tired and cross after coping all day. And I am delighted to see the best of reality after whatever bureaucratic foolishness has gone on at the studio.

Of course there are other times, too. Times when it's a great effort to enjoy their chatter, really to pay attention, when I'd rather just sit quietly and unwind. And there are times of feeling guilty, too, of wondering if this is fair. "Am I giving enough of myself to my husband and children. Or am I being truly selfish? Is it worthwhile?" For me, these other times come infrequently enough that I can say it is worthwhile.

For those of us who have decided it is worth the effort, the next question is "How." How does a woman raise children, take care of a husband, manage a house, laundry, garden, dinner parties, cats, correspondence—and hold a paid job? I'm convinced there's a Parkinsonian answer: in a given time, it is possible to do as much as you have to do, or as much as you want to do. This brings me back to the point I made at the beginning of this essay, about the difference in quality of time between the at-home and the out-to-work mother. Out-to-work imposes organization on your time, divides it into predictable chunks, and makes it not only possible but imperative to plan ahead. You will shop once a week, so you write out a weeks' menus in detail and do not wait for inspiration to strike in the supermarket. Commuting time is excellent for this and all the other lists you will find yourself making. Lists become a major preoccupation; reminders for yourself and everyone else. I know that things are getting out of hand when I find myself making lists of the lists I have to make.

All those hints in the ladies' magazines become practical necessities: never put clothes away with buttons off or hems torn—you will be in too great a hurry to fix it in the morning; decide what to wear before you go to sleep—in the quiet of the night you will remember which blouse is at the cleaner; beauty routines must be real routines—you can't go to work in curlers.

A little laziness doesn't hurt, either. The woman with a lazy streak will keep basic cleaning equipment on each floor of her house, saving time and steps. She will sort and fold the laundry by individuals as it comes out of the dryer, and, when she carries it upstairs, she will carry down the wastebaskets. She will always cook a double recipe—one for dinner, one for the freezing compartment. She will assign jobs to the children, and hopefully, they will be a real help. She will develop a sense of priorities, and the important things will get done.

"How" to go out to work doesn't start with this sort of organizational know-how. That is learned on the job. "How" starts with an enthusiastic husband. Frank Jordan was in favor of my going back to work, interested in what I was doing, and convinced I should be a) put in charge, or failing that, b) paid what he thought I was worth. He is not what you'd call long suffering, but he'll defend my right to go off to work—even though it costs him money— so long as he has clean shirts, a good breakfast, and his socks properly sorted. His patience and support are vital to this kind of life: not only helping me over rough spots, but also coloring the children's attitude about my working.

If an enthusiastic family is one prime requisite, competent help is the other. This is the stickiest wicket of all. To find someone in whom you have complete confidence is first of all difficult, and second, liable to cost as much as you can earn. I've tried two solutions—the housekeeper and the babysitter—and each has its advantages. The first year, I hired, for the television season, a warm and wonderful woman who lived in from Monday to Friday. This made life very easy for me. I knew the children were getting affectionate care and attention, and since Maria was a meticulous and energetic housekeeper, everything was sparkling, and when I got home I could look forward to a good dinner with no cleaning up afterward. Lovely! Frank and I have always done a good deal of entertaining, and with this happy set-up, there was no reason to cut down on it. Relying on those ubiquitous lists I mentioned, it was possible to plan dinner parties during the odd five minutes at work, knowing that when the guests arrived, the house, children, silver, and so on were as elegant as could be.

Although easy, having a live-in housekeeper was far too expensive. *Not* counting the money I spent on clothes and shoes, I figured a profit of a hundred dollars for seven months work.

The following season we had a babysitter. Again, we were fortunate to find someone affectionate and energetic. Mrs. P. came in at noon, when the children got home from nursery school, and stayed until I got home. Flexibility was terribly important, as television hours are anything but regular. Mrs. P. did no cooking, and no ironing, but kept the house very well, and encouraged me to leave the dinner dishes for her to do when she came. All in all, a most satisfactory arrangement, and although I paid her more than regular babysitting rates, working this way was financially feasible.

The money advantage aside, working with a babysitter is much more difficult. There is much more house- and kitchen-work to do when you come home, and there is a psychological difference as well: the housekeeper, because she has much more authority, takes over the minor decision-making and assumes some initiative; the babysitter, competent as she may be, keeps hoping you'll come home and get her off the hook.

A word about nursery school. It seems a good thing to me, not because of the "socializing process" or "learning to adjust to one's peer group"—gregarious children with neighborhood playmates learn these things more or less easily—but because going off to school makes it simpler for the children to understand papa going off to the office and mama going off to the studio. Then, too, nursery school provides the sort of organized, creative play that you would be supervising if you were home, and which you really can't expect a professional housekeeper to undertake. This, too, is an expense, and if you otherwise would not be sending your child to nursery school, you must include these costs in the cost of going out to work.

Complicated, yes. Expensive, yes. Demanding, yes. But it can all be done and it will work somehow, if you and your husband want it to.

The foregoing covers to some extent what I do, why I do it, and how I am able to go out to work. There is one more question, and that is So What? What happens to a woman who is work cum wife/mother oriented when she's not working?

For the past year, I have not been working in television, owing mainly to a major house remodeling. Even the most devoted household help would balk at cooking in the fireplace, and fixing the gallons of coffee necessary to fuel carpenters. It did not seem wise to me to leave the children in the rubble and noise and confusion. So I turned down the Young People's Concerts with regret. And what has happened since? Ego-bending as it is, it must be admitted that television didn't suffer without me.

The first few weeks were bliss. I planted bulbs, fixed breakfast in my bathrobe, wrote letters, cleaned closets, tried new recipes. Then my friends found out I was home. Since I was not working, they—and I, too—assumed I had lots of free time. Why not help form a new conservation group? or collect for the United Fund? take on just a few hours of volunteer work? accept a school alumnae job? did—and in the end found myself spending at least the work on a village committee? So you do—or at least I did—and in the end found myself spending at least the amount of time formerly spent at my job on a confusing diffusion of civic and volunteer projects. All of them important and needing to be done, but much more difficult for me. Difficult because I find it very hard to work well with fragments of time, and almost impossible to think of more than one thing at a time. Paid work, with its organized chunks of time, fits my habit of mind, and makes me turn my lazy side to good use. Juggling the fragments of several projects, committees, housework leads to just one end: procrastination. No priority system makes sense to me when my calendar looks like a manic tic-tac-toe. Writing this, for example, has resulted in the weeks' laundry—clean and dirty—being piled helter-skelter in baskets all over our bedroom. For once, I have been grateful to have my husband away.

The answer? I don't know. But it is election year again, and Frank Jordan will be away a great deal, and F. D. and Mieux are healthy and happy and doing well in school . . . and I'd surely like to work on another political campaign.

14

EILEEN DIAZ

Finding My Old Self in a Larger World

Eileen Diaz is presently a Coordinator for a Community Action Program. She has worked in community social services since her marriage; before her marriage she combined social work with free-lance writing. Born in Italy and the child of immigrants, she graduated from college in the late 1940s. She has three school-age children, and has worked since the youngest was two.

When I was a child my mother often told me of her only memory of her own mother. I had listened with a nebulous dread creeping over me as she described a vision of her mother going to work, passing out of a wrought iron gate in front of their home, as though the scene had been a prelude to her coming untimely death. My mother and father had emigrated from Italy and their memories were interwoven with a great nostalgia and a sense of loss. When my mother went out to work during the depression, although it was for a few months, I wonder if I relived this sadness which my mother's experience had made a part of me. If so, I have no memory of it, but thinking of it re-creates for me my own feelings when the expenses of a growing family and my own need to be back in the world of ideas and action outside of the family circle, combined to make me a working mother. Memories drift back of my youngest son, then about two, sobbing at the door, begging me not to leave, of disturbing fantasies of possible injuries, physical and psychological, which could occur that filled my mind traveling to and from work. I remember my horror when the children told me that one babysitter had chased them around the apartment and had playfully stuck pins in them when they had misbehaved. She also had put them all in the bathtub, herself included, for a community bath fun-time.

My adjustment to leaving the children and resolving my guilt feelings because I was, on one level, relieved to be away from the endless routine of child care and house cleaning, took time. Although being a mother was a joy and fulfillment, as time passed I realized that I needed some other interest. My communication with an adult world had been very limited and I went back to work with almost as much relish as others might go to a social evening.

In all this slush of feelings, separation, guilt, and anxiety, there emerged the clear intellectual evaluation with which I assured myself that I was doing the right thing; and strangely enough, this sustained me until I did manage to conquer most of my negative feelings. True, I often came home an exhausted, uninterested, harassed, screeching ugly, but I also felt a deepening appreciation for the children and on weekends tried even harder to compensate by special excursions, and wanted very much to be with them. We had fun and I felt like a more interesting person to have around. There was also more money with which to do things. A working mother feels the pressure put on her concerning her duty to her children. As a mother she is expected to devote herself to her children's well-being. If she goes out to work to help herself, provide a greater measure of the necessities of life for the family, and to help the children on their way to independence, she is still thought of by some as less of a good mother. This is based on the assumption that the good mother is one who is constantly on her children's trail and sharing every possible moment of living with them. Depending on the family income, where the family lives, and the cultural environment, this varies, but often there is a certain amount of disfavor for the mother who does not have direct care of her children as a full-time job.

Substitute mothers are hard to find. I think my greatest success was with my 79-year-old father who "retired" to care for his house and garden and was glad to be helpful by babysitting. He played baseball with them (the boys ran the bases for him) and he became "grandpa" to a variety of neighborhood children. This was a delightful arrangement until the trip into Manhattan became too tiresome for him and I reached the fortuitous point in life when I was able to arrange my hours of work to coincide with the children's time in school. One of the ways we can respond to the needs of working mothers is to provide jobs for women with school-age children for the hours that they are in school, or if not, to provide suitable day care and after school programs. The public day-care centers in New York City are run by the Department of Social Services (Welfare) and have endless waiting lists. Any "intact" family where there is income is almost automatically excluded because priority is given to women on public assistance or who would be if they could not work. The private nurseries are expensive and sparse. These services are for a limited age group although there are some facilities for older children after school. Suitable babysitters are not easy to find, and are much more expensive if you expect them to take care of the children in your own home. A new plan has been devised for women on public assistance or in a family with low income in which certain homes are licensed so that the mother may care for a specified number of children. The mothers whose children are cared for can enter training courses or work. The plan has many deficiencies from the point of view of providing the children with the most beneficial environment while the mother is at work.

One of my problems in returning to work was the onset of fatigue and the lack of energy I experienced often as I tried to cope with family responsibilities after an eight-hour work day. I had a series of jobs which taxed my strength, with anti-poverty community action pro-grams, a settlement house, and a pilot youth program. My duties varied from group work with teenagers in a ghetto area "coffee-house" experiment to running a health services program. I organized action committees, co-ordinated voter-registration drives, developed a cultural arts program, supervised employment counselors, worked with elementary school children in group recreation pro-grams, and for a time ran a housing clinic. Working in one poverty area and living in East Harlem exposed me to many challening and exhausting situations. Helping in emergencies such as fires and acute illnesses were all part of a day's work. The frustration of being able to do relatively little in the face of problems such as deteriorated housing, rats preying on children, and the all too familiar list of hard core agonies of our cities, was an occupational

hazard. These experiences also gave me an enriching involvement in the lives of people outside of the immediate
family which gave my life a new dimension and brought
me back to the work which had been so important to
me before marriage. I had spent years working in East
Harlem since college days when I started to teach cat-
echism in an old Catholic church which was a converted
bathhouse, and returned later with a friend to open a
store front children's center. Later we moved into the
neighborhood to extend our work. My association with
the Catholic Worker movement left its mark on my conscience so that when years later I returned to work, I
was happy to be a part of the struggle for social and
economic justice. Although my motivation now is not
religious and I do work as well to earn money, I feel
more at ease with myself because of this involvement.

To compare the plus values of working to the minus is
difficult. Looking back to the days I worked full-time I
remember the nights I came home tired and served a
thrown together meal. I remember talks with the children
when I listed all the advantages of my working and heard
them agree that having money to spend on things they
wanted and activities was worth the sacrifices. I was developing an apologia entitled "Mother Should Work."
There was the fear that my working reflected on their
father's image as breadwinner, aggravated by his problems
with seasonal employment and relatively low wages, and
the subtle and not so subtle obstacles in his path as a first
generation Puerto Rican immigrant. Some resentments
arose and were not entirely resolved. He was raised in a
culture where men's work is clearly defined and they expect the woman's role in the family to continue smoothly
whether or not she is working. Although he was never
opposed to my working and the economic advantages were

clear, his occasional dissatisfactions were indications that it wasn't the best of all possible arrangements under which we were living. I had no help with the housework and meals so I was never in the mood for any criticism. My dependence on him lessened and in a way my individuality and personality were strengthened by my life outside the home. I felt livelier and more like "my old self" in that my life was not as constrained by immovable limitations. I think our relationship actually improved.

The role of women in marriage and in society is undergoing change. In our everyday lives many of us are redefining the family. Women want the freedom to make full use of their talents as persons as well as mothers. They want to participate fully in all fields of human effort and creativity. This may not necessitate as much a change in the role of women as it means removing barriers to their becoming adult in the greater society as well as within the family. When I think about the past years of combining work and home, I feel a sense of satisfaction at having overcome some family problems by going out to work. The new problems which arose I resolved reasonably well. My children are proud of me and the responsibilities I have at work. They learned to reach out to other people without ceasing to be close to me, have many interests, and positive attitudes toward school and recreation. Disclaiming objectivity, I think they are great. I found many of the fears about harmful effects to marriage, children, and home were exaggerated by my own insecurity about going back to work. The advantages I had being a college graduate and having had work experience helped. It was not difficult for me to find work. After finding work I had the benefit of working with people who put human values first and did not put undue pressure on me concerning time off for serious illnesses at home, arrangements of work schedules, coming in late on days when one of the children was in a class play or needed a special visit to the doctor. These are considerations not all workers share. Factory workers forced to work overtime and otherwise pressured by employers are at a disadvantage. The rule is, "You want to work—pay the price." Often working mothers break down under the strain, especially those who have to tune themselves to a power sewing machine or busy switchboard, work which may be depersonalized, done in an atmosphere which is punitive and demanding. The question of work, and its relation to the person, is one which has been studied and discussed but the knowledge gained has not been applied to our economic system. Man is still made for work and not work for man. Much of our effort is wasted while work which is needed is left undone, such as the rebuilding of slums, extending health care, and revitalizing our schools.

Women need to organize their political and moral strength behind a more realistic use of the work force of both sexes. We need to rebel against meaningless work, against work which is destructive to the building of world peace, dehumanizing work, and see to it that whatever power we have is exerted towards our personal good and the common good. We must reject any economic system based on war and dependent on war for its health.

Employment for women is being encouraged if they are recipients of public funds. There is a growing rancor being expressed towards dependent mothers and an eagerness to get them off the welfare rolls and into the labor market. Although this may eventually benefit the women involved, one would hope that the original purposes of the aid, the protection of the children, should be considered, as well as the woman's capability of handling two jobs at once, and her own evaluation of where her best interest and that of her children lies. At times it seems that the fundamental ethical value that a person has a right to life and what is needed to maintain life as a dignified free individual has been lost. One of the reasons for these fatherless homes is the system which does not provide wages at the level needed to maintain families and which is run with an underclass of minority groups who, if employed, are doing the menial, clean-up, back-breaking, dead-end jobs, and an inferior educational system which makes further advancement impossible without years of remediation or extensive training. If there were more emphasis placed on creating meaningful, well-paying jobs for men, especially the urban and rural poor and minority groups who have faced institutionalized discrimination in employment for decades, many of the resultant social ills would be cured. Work for women is important in that in the present reality for many individuals and families, it is a step out of poverty. It is also important as a creative outlet. Society benefits from the talent and skills of working women. Making it easier for women who do work to satisfy their children's needs, escape the deadly effects of overwork and emotional strain, is a goal we should set for ourselves. Increasing the number of day-care services, after school programs, and making more part-time jobs available are ways of helping. From my own experience, I prefer nursery school care for the preschool group. Children under two are best cared for by their mothers unless there is serious financial or emotional need, and no other way to resolve the problem. Since each woman is different it must be an individual decision. I experienced a lessening of anxiety as my own children grew older. My children, now ten, nine, and six experienced more visible insecurity at younger

ages although I did not work when they were infants,
except when the first child was about one and my husband
was in the hospital. I worked for about three months and
was overwhelmed when my son became seriously ill with
measles. Rushing from work, to baby, to hospital, I became completely drained. As soon as my husband was
back at work I stopped. I didn't work again until my
third child was about two. This conflict of duties is most
acute when the children are sick. If they are seriously
ill, there is no question, I stay home. If the serious symp-
toms disappear and I am reasonably sure there is no
danger I go to work without much anxiety but there is
no denying that often when the situation is unclear, I
feel insecure as to what decision is best. Fortunately, their
health is good and it's the usual run of viruses or childhood diseases that occur. Then there are those playground
accidents. My six-year-old son cut his hand tumbling in
the playground while I was at work. He had to have seven
stitches in his hand. When I got home he was very upset
and I joined him. You can't help but think that if you
were there you could have prevented it. Sometimes the
accidents happen in front of you and in the home, but
worry about the safety of children is very much a problem
for mothers who work. I have a neighbor who works near
home and who is terrified when she hears a fire engine.
I remember when I first started working an old rhyme
kept running through my head,

"Ladybug, ladybug, fly away home,
    Your house is on fire, and your children will burn."

Is this neurotic or realistic? A little of both I think. In
neighborhoods like ours, fires are commonplace. In the
apartment we lived in before we moved to a housing

project there was a series of small fires started by defective wiring. Mothers are instinctively protective and these worries are very real. My son was lost for a few hours at Rockaway Beach one summer while on a day-camp trip. I waited tensely until I got word that he was safe at the police station where he was found by relieved counselors. Incidents like these happen whether or not you are at home but a mother at work feels more anxious about such things. Children also carefully compare their lives to their friends' and one of mine asked me why I couldn't stay home all day like their mother. Interestingly, when their close friends' mother got a job they came to regard mothers' working as a state of normalcy and progressed to bragging about it.

When I first thought of going back to work it was with a lack of confidence in my ability. The thought of getting through a work day and coming home to do most of the things that kept me busy at home all day was frightening. With some encouragement, I aimed high, pulled myself together and found a temporary, well-paying job with which to experiment. When I began to work at a perm-anent job I realized I would have to accept certain hard-ships but they were tempered by an enjoyment of my work and the good things which grew out of it. Battling fatigue and illness at times, I learned to be more con-fident about my ability to find suitable work and arrange my schedule so that much of the strain was eliminated. I am convinced that mothers who work should not settle into a 35- to 40-hour-a-week work schedule unless they are very energetic types and should do their best to avoid urban rush hours and otherwise conserve themselves. We are a long way from making this possible for the majority of women with children, especially in low-income families where there is a corresponding low educational level, lack of work experience, work skills, and often language skills. These are the families which need immediate plans for more part-time paid remediation classes and job training with opportunities for professional training as well. More important than this is that we resolve the problem of male youth and adults who are now unemployed or underemployed and who have little hope of ever earning enough to support a family in all its basic needs. This is our first priority in the area of work. It calls for radical changes in the attitudes and wills of government and industry as to their responsibilities.

15

BRIGITTE BERGER

A Career and a Traditional Household Can Go Together

Brigitte Berger is a professor of sociology teaching full-time. She now has two young boys and has been continuously active in her career. A committed professional worker, she still emphasizes high standards of domestic life. A more traditional family style can also be combined with the continuous full-time employment of the mother.

Wherever I turn, I encounter the "modern woman." Next to the war in Vietnam, the "frightening aspects of urban life," and the hippies, she seems to be the most frequently discussed topic in present-day America, competing only with the somewhat more titillating subject of sex, which, by rights, also falls into her domain. The common notions about the "modern woman" are so diverse and controversial that I have been moved to inquire more precisely "who is this modern woman that nearly everyone should be so mindful of her?" I am told—and here, for once, there seems to be a general agreement—that she is a woman come of age, independent economically and intellectually, active, rational, cool, determined, and self-assured; she is world-conquering woman, whose residual insecurities cannot be battened by anyone even though she is susceptible to the blandishments of psychoanalysts. She is no longer a part of the traditional order but a sovereign creator of her world. And, depending upon the location of the respective evaluator in relation to her, this is either thought to be a marvellous step forward in woman's long march for subjugation and slavery to freedom and emancipation or a terrible development endangering the emotional demands and the need for stability in married life and in the family.

As a professional sociologist, however, I still am searching for data on the "modern woman." She is barely known to empirical sociology, and she makes only a marginal impact on the Gallup polls, which more usually document her gullibility, illogicality, insecurity, and contradictory behavior. Personally, I think that although this magnificent creature of a "modern woman" may exist, I certainly am not one. If evaluated in the above terms, I probably could be called an old-fashioned, conventional woman who has come to terms with the admittedly extraordinary demands of a combined family and professional life in a rather traditional manner. These old-fashioned qualities may strike the reader as somewhat anachronistic in modern times. However, in my case, these qualities and standards have helped me tremendously and I wholeheartedly recommend them to the consideration of any professional woman who wants to lead a satisfying family life, or better, the other way around, to the wife and mother who also wants to pursue a career.

The modern woman is generally thought to have a real freedom of determination about her future career, which she will plan for and aim at unerringly and persistently. She sets out and gets the right education and then she unfolds her potential. Things were completely different with me. For at least nine years after I had left Junior College in Europe, I wandered about geographically and intellectually, switching from one subject to the other, from one area of occupation and profession to the next without being able to make up my mind what I wanted or even could do. My efforts and attention shifted from becoming an architect to opening an art gallery on the Island of Capri, from starting a publishing house for children's literature to running a poultry farm, from becoming the mayor of a small village and thus launching upon a splendid career in politics to marrying a diplomat and engaging in politics on a different scale. I worked as a secretary, a court-stenographer, as a librarian. I taught school and for a few months I even traveled with a puppet theater.

This is by no means an exhaustive list of my adventures in the "purposeful and unerring progress" towards a professional career. When I finally entered the field of sociology, almost by accident, my fancy for and my dedication to the field developed only gradually and that only after some setbacks and hard work. When I was very close to my Ph.D., I still wanted to change toward a different area. But by then it had become impractical and I continued my work in sociology. To this day, I never have regretted this decision. I truly enjoy my profession. The point I think needs emphasizing here is that a woman can come to a career also at a later point in her life and that a career does not need to be planned and organized in a cool, rational manner beforehand in order to be meaningful and satisfying. From a sociologist, this may sound paradoxical, but my experience gives some indication, at least to me, that there are probably many more accidental aspects involved in a woman's choice of her career than are usually thought.

This latter point is also relevant when it comes to the discussion of marriage. In a recent symposium on American Woman in Science and Engineering, one of the speakers gave the all-important counsel to career women: be careful to choose the right husband. An image of the "modern woman" was invoked, who sits down and makes a list of all the qualities of the applicant for marriage, carefully and rationally balancing off the various pros and cons and thereby ultimately arriving at an intelligent solution, which could almost be called "scientific." In theory this sounds like excellent advice, worthwhile for every woman to follow.

From my professional and personal experiences, I have the feeling that this vision of the modern woman who views marriage with a cold and dispassionate eye is still far off. For one, a professional and intellectual woman in general has a much smaller chance of getting married than a nonprofessional woman. That is to say, her field of choice is limited by definition and if she wants marriage, she may very well be forced into compromises. Furthermore, I think that our success in marriage prediction scales are still rather inadequate and in any case, probably not applicable to intellectual women, that is, those who are likely to pursue a career.

I married a man completely different from the one a marriage prediction scale would recommend for me. I married him because he entertained me and interested me intellectually, a man to whom I could talk for hours without ever being bored for a second, knowing well that difficulties could arise. Much to my surprise there were many fewer difficulties and problems than I had apprehended and which I was led to expect on the basis of professional counselling data.

During the first years of marriage, we had no children and although I worked in addition to completing my Ph.D., I had enough leisure to run my little household smoothly. I had ample time to give my full attention to my husband and his interests. During these years I learned a most important lesson, which became the basis for the years after the children arrived. I could observe in the cases of other so-called intellectual couples the devastating effect of marriage and children upon both husband and wife, if one does not counteract these effects energetically. Let me illustrate these effects briefly: The women of my acquaintance were, in general, not prepared for tackling the organization of a household efficiently in addition to the even more tiring demands small children made upon their lives. As a result, they became helpless, weary, nervous, and simply exhausted. This general state of pressure was further increased by their own intellectual needs and their desire to keep in touch with the outside world.

The husbands, of course, were in principle much better off. They, at least, could escape the turmoil and the pressing demands of the household by simply removing themselves to their place of work. However, even they usually could not escape the fate marital life had in store for them. Once they got home in the evening, or earlier—depending upon the type of work—a regular persecution set in for their attention, their help, their commiseration. The men who follow an intellectual or artistic profession, a profession which they usually carry out at home, are the real sufferers. Here, husbands are often reduced to the station of an inexpensive and convenient household helper. In one case I remember the husband not only had to wash the windows, wash the dishes, help bathe and feed the children, but he also had to wash the diapers his exhausted wife simply did not get around to doing.

The charming, gay, and hopeful young wives became bitter, disillusioned, and frantic, full of resentment against their husbands and life in general. The housekeeping, at best, was haphazard and disorganized, with dirty laundry on the bathroom floor, unpolished glasses in the cupboard, books, letters, and magazines scattered all over the house. The children, God bless them, somehow always managed to make their demands felt and were the real gainers in this turbidity. But clearly, both partners suffer greatly from the state of marriage when they have intellectual ambitions. This situation is so well-known, that anyone can fill in more details.

I made up my mind in the early years of marriage, if at all possible, not to fall prey to this trap of marriage. And even though it has been extremely hard at times, I think I circumvented at least these particular pitfalls. I decided that housekeeping was my chore and not that of my husband. I further decided to organize and run my household well without becoming fanatical. I feel that a well-run, neat and comfortable house is of tremendous importance, especially in the marriage of professional couples. I am convinced that any woman, if need be, can organize and manage a household adequately; under pressure she will be driven to excel. Once she has learned this, she will manage.

Never shy away from work, buckle down and do it— now. What has to be done, has to be done, and waiting certainly will not help. If you have help in the household —and if you work and have children, you must have help —never depend upon her mercy and initiative. If you cannot show her how things have to be done and how quickly they can be done, she will not know what is expected of her. If you are a sloppy housekeeper, your help usually becomes sloppy, even though she has been known to perform better elsewhere. Another thing I learned is that the intellectually oriented woman can be the best of cooks, if she so wants to be. Cooking can serve as a hobby and relaxing pastime. I am firmly convinced that cooking is largely a matter of phantasy and imagination— and here certainly the intellectual woman excels. Supper, the one big meal of the day in the life of working couples, can and should become a time for everyone to look forward to. External influences of good food and drink can do so much for the general well-being of everyone in the family.

This brings me to the organization of family life. I am a strong believer in reserving specific periods of the day and evening for life and activities of the entire family. Clearly, when you work, the only time left free is breakfast and suppertime with the evening to follow. If at all possible, we plan no outside activities for the evening. Instead we like to invite guests to our house and I gladly take on the extra work of entertainment, if I don't have to leave the house. In general, I like an early supper so that some time will be left afterwards to play with the children before they go to bed. An early supper gives us the opportunity for an extended family life.

Yet these are not the most crucial questions in the life of the professional woman. With the advent of children the problem arises whether she should devote herself to the task of bringing up "high-quality" children, to use the somewhat unfortunate phrase of the sociologist Talcott Parsons, instead of simply having them. Implied in this question is a peculiar understanding of the role of the modern woman, namely that she has to give up her interest, her career, and herself for the sake of her children. Also implied in this question is the notion that the mother's total devotion to her children would be beneficial for them. I have always doubted the validity of this widespread notion and I have still to see empirical data which would prove this understanding to be relevant.

Speaking for myself, I feel rather strongly that I would be a much more impatient mother than I am now, if I were not working. I do think that in spite of the many obstacles and difficulties that have to be overcome and that can be overcome, husbands, children, and women themselves benefit greatly if the mother has outside interests and a professional world of her own. When I come home from work, I look impatiently forward to seeing husband and children, playing with them, listening to their problems. I also look forward to taking care of the children's physical needs, for instance, giving them their bath, checking their clothes, and so on. Because I have spent hours in the pursuit of my work, in the course of which I have become exhausted intellectually, interaction with my children restores my strength. I am always happy to see that instead of being worn out by them during a long day with them, I am always patient and revitalized by them after a day of work in my profession.

Of course, practical problems will always turn up, and very much, indeed, depends upon the way in which we solve them. The mere fact that I have to be out of the house for hours at a stretch makes it necessary that provisions be made for having the housework done and the children cared for. This is the tiresome and unpleasant topic of domestic help. By now I could write a sad as well as entertaining book on that. A string of female faces comes to my mind, ranging from a literally mad Icelandic woman to a whole group of beautiful, gentle Haitian girls who took turns at showing up in unpredicted numbers and sequences at my house, from man-hunting Europeans to ineffective Americans. Each one of these faces represents in my memory not only the help they have rendered to me, but much more the problems they created.

After years of experience I have come to the conclusion that there exists probably no one woman or girl who can meet all of your expectations and needs. I have given up this search. I have also come to realize that no matter how good the person is who takes care of your children, you will never be satisfied. My solution to this general problem is that I now willingly spend much more money on help than I ever expected to, because I simply cannot constantly be bothered and annoyed with domestic help problems. It is energy and emotion consuming. I also am dividing functions, whereby I employ separate persons for housework and for child care. The housekeeper knows her work and can carry it out without being constantly disturbed by the children's demands. The nurse-maid or "Nanny" problem is still an open one. I have found in general that younger girls are better for smaller children. They are still close enough in age to really enjoy playing foolish little games and having a "rough" time with them.

Another quality I personally find absolutely essential in the young woman who lives in my house and devotes herself to my children, is that she have some intellectual awareness and interests. We find it simply unbearable to sit with a stranger at the breakfast and supper table with whom we cannot talk. I, for one, find it impossible to talk, for instance, with a young girl who has only cosmetics, clothes, and boys in her mind. One of my best experiences was with a young European girl of simple background who was obsessed by a craving for knowledge. She not only marched my little ones to and through every museum in New York frequently, but she also took time to inform herself in detail about how the children's individual needs could best be met. Moreover, she became a real friend of the family and of our friends too. Her intellectual interests made her a genuine addition to our household; on the other hand, her intellectual interests also took her away from us again.

Let me say, finally, a few things about the influence of my family life upon my work. If you ask me whether my family interferes with my work I must say, "Of course they do." Here I was forced to come to a real compromise. I have decided that my family comes first and my work comes second, and only third in line, am I myself. Small children make it necessary for the working mother to curtail her outside activities. In my case, this means that I cannot go off to meetings, conventions or take occupational trips. It means that my professional career probably progresses much more slowly than it would if I were not married. I still have not finished the book for which I made a contract almost two years ago, but I know I shall finish it some time. But I have managed always to work full-time, even when pregnant. Yet I also know that the immediate demands my small children make upon my time will decrease when they are growing up. But I do not wish to hurry this process.

I always find it paradoxical when the nonworking mothers of small children go to great pains to arrange the social life of the preschool set. This will inevitably diminish the influence of the family in favor of the influence of the peer group at a very early age. I feel rather strongly that as long as I have a chance to mold and influence my children I will do so; the peer group will take over soon enough. I do not wish to imply that I have found *the* secret to the right education of my children. We are blessed with two extraordinarily difficult little boys who keep me very humble, indeed. I only wish to emphasize that from my point of view the family has to keep control of the influences of the world upon children, especially in their early years.

This means professionally that my time is limited. When it comes to the needs of myself as a physical person, my time is even more limited. It has become next to impossible for me to give careful attention to my image as a woman of "fashion." The time is simply not there, even though nostalgic feelings come up once in a while. Even so, I would not do anything to change this situation. When at a recent party people were asked if they would be given a choice to be someone else, everyone but me admitted to a longing for a different profession, a different life, a different century. I, if given a choice, would choose this very same life, because I like it. It is rough sailing at times, but I would not like to miss any of it.

16

SUSAN GORDON, M.D.

I Want Excellence in Both Work and Family Life

Dr. Susan Gordon is a physician who teaches pediatrics to other doctors and medical students. She has been committed to her profession from before her marriage and worked continuously while having her four children, two of whom are now teenagers. She has made many adjustments in both her career and family life for the sake of both; she reflects on the strains and satisfactions of pursuing excellence in two directions simultaneously.

Q:[1] Tell me your name and how many children you have.

A: My name is Susan Gordon; I have four children.

[1] This account of the experience of combining work and child rearing was written from a personal interview. Both the interviews and the essays in this book derived from the questionnaire which appears in the Appendix.

The two boys are seventeen and fourteen, and the girls are twelve and eight.

Q: What kind of work do you do?

A: I'm a physician with a specialty in pediatrics and I am in what is called academic pediatrics which means going back to medical school and being a teacher, a teacher of medical students and house staff, interns and residents.

Q: How much time does it take?

A: Oh, it's a full-time job. I leave home in the morning about 8 or 8:30 and come home by 6 or 6:30, five days a week.

Q: Did you choose this as being even less demanding than a private practice?

A: Yes, it actually is. The commuting gets a little tiring but it's pleasant really; the parkway has no commercial traffic. So it is not too difficult; and the teaching hospital is uptown, so that the traffic problem is not overwhelming. Before I become overwhelmed with it I'm there.

Q: Do you think it is worth it to live out in the suburbs?

A: It is for me. One of the reasons is that I was born and brought up in the country and I don't like the city. I tolerated it for four years but I really could not live in the city for any length of time, so that I have to put up with the two-hour-a-day commute.

Q: You say you were born in the country. Were you born in a family in which your mother worked?

A: No, my mother did not work except during World War II when she worked as a duty for the war. Of course I was already a teenager at that time and I was the youngest of a family of four children. But that was the only kind of work she did; she didn't even do her own housework.

Q: What was your attitude, as you grew up, toward a

woman's role? You're a doctor, which takes quite a great deal of ambition and interest. Did you always want to be a doctor?

A: Since about the age of ten, I had decided I was going to be either a doctor or a social worker. I remember I had a Red Cross first aid book which interested me greatly and I decided then that I wanted to be a doctor. My motivation for going into medicine was primarily a humanitarian one, if you wish to call it that, doing something for other people.

Q: What was your parents' reaction to the fact that you wanted to be a doctor?

A: They thought it was fine. They encouraged me. Women were equal to men, so to speak, in our household; we were certainly free to pursue the career we wanted. I was the only one of the girls who did choose a career, but I got wholehearted support. There was no problem.

Q: Was there any idea that this might conflict with your other feminine role later?

A: No, because at that stage in my life I was determined never to get married. I felt that if I was to serve humanity, marriage was not for me; I thought I couldn't mix the two. I suppose it was partly a cover-up. I didn't have too many boyfriends. I was a bookworm and so I just said, "Well I'm not interested."

Q: How long did that last?

A: I went on through prep school, college and still said that, until about my senior year in college, then I didn't say much about it any more.

Q: Did you go to a girls' school?

A: Yes I did.

Q: Did you have any difficulty getting into medical school as a woman?

A: Some, yes. I applied to several of the major ones

and they turned me down. I was not a science major. I was an economics and sociology major and despite the fact that medical schools claimed they were very interested in people who were not pure science majors they accepted the biology and chemisty majors before they accepted the social science majors.

Q: And being a woman as well?

A: And being a woman. Finally I was accepted at Women's Medical College. And I went off there, in the fall of '46.

Q: And you completed your course there?

A: No, because in the summer of '46 I met my future husband and decided you could easily mix the two! During my third year of medical school we were married and I transferred to the school where he was assistant dean of men.

Q: He was already established?

A: He was already established and I finished my medical schooling there.

Q: At the very beginning your husband knew that he was getting someone who wanted to go to school and be a doctor. What was his attitude?

A: Fine. He was all for it. By the end of that summer we had planned to have four children—two boys and two girls. I think I had wanted six and he said no let's try for four. We had the names picked out and we had decided to establish a child health and guidance clinic in some needy place. I would be the medical director and he would be the psychologist. That would be our life's work.

Q: How were you going to work the children with the two careers? Did you think about this at all?

A: Well, I don't think at that point we talked about anything as concrete as how this was going to work out. It just was.

Q: So you had to finish first, before you began your

family. I take it that you had no religious problems with family planning.

A: No. We had none at all. We have a completely planned family. We missed a little bit toward the end when we couldn't conceive Johanna when we wanted to. She was a little bit late, but it was a totally planned family. So we had no problems. After I finished my internship we decided to have the first child, which meant that I became pregnant during my internship. The first was born in August and I finished my internship July 1st. They are all summer babies for this very reason. The next one was born at the end of residency, in early September. And the next one was born during vacation in private practice, and the fourth one was born after I had gone back to the medical center to do part-time teaching.

Q: I see the summer pattern.

A: Summers are important because we had decided that one of the best things we could do for the kids was for me to take summers off, not just one month but two.

Q: From the very beginning of your career you did this then?

A: Yes.

Q: This was one of your concessions then?

A: Right. At least six weeks, if not the whole two months.

Q: I see. Well, now when you had the first child, what arrangements did you make? Did you go right back to work?

A: Well, not with the first child and I think this was a mistake. It might be something for young mothers coming along who have careers to think about. We were of course, all tied up with those psychologists including psychiatrists like Freud, I suppose, who felt that the formative years of a child emotionally are the first three to five years of life. Therefore, perhaps it was important

for me to have been home for the first year. So the first
year after the first child was born I took off the whole
year with some exception. I volunteered to work almost
as a resident about two or three days a week. I guess I
was there most of the day for about three days a week.
So that I was essentially not pursuing my career at that
point, but just sort of keeping myself interested and
keeping my finger in the pot. Then I went back to full-
time training which was residency training when he was
about a year old and completed that. I think one should
do all one can as far as training is concerned if this is
what has to be done when you have very young children.
When they are very young, they don't miss you as much.

Q: Did you miss them when you left? Did you have
conflicts about leaving? What arrangements did you make?

A: I hate to say this but I never had conflicts about
leaving babies. And as I have gotten more experience in
the field of pediatrics I've found that as long as a baby
has a loving hand to feed it, to change it, to hold it, to
kiss it, to do whatever needs to be done as far as physical
contact is concerned (and of course you can do this yourself after you get home), the baby doesn't have very much
to worry about. He doesn't grow up with some terrible
emotional problem, I don't think. But when he gets
aware enough to know that you are leaving and it's a
pretty long day without you, when he says as you go out
the door take me with you, or he gets an old pocketbook
of yours and puts it on his arm and says I'm going too,
then you begin to feel terrible. You sort of grit your teeth
and realize that five minutes later he's occupied, occupied
with the purse or some other substitute and he's fine. It's
only the first couple of minutes of the separation that
they really mind. Still, at that age I began to have some
qualms. Also, when the children would say to me on my
supposed day off from private practice, "You were sup-

posed to be off today and be with us," and the telephone would ring. That got to me, and I thought, well they're right. Actually when I found that in private practice I was leaving home at 9:00 after having been at telephone hour from 7:30 to 8:30 and not getting back until 11:00 at night, something had to be done. Then I went back to work to teach part-time. And that was very successful.

Q: Part of my question was what arrangements did you make about your career and mother substitutes?

A: We were in New York City when our first child was born; we were there for almost the first three years of his life. We had a woman that we had hired through an ad in the paper who turned out to be an excellent person. She was a very good mother substitute, a very warm person who loved our child. Ted was the first one, and she took very good care of him. My husband was absolutely marvelous. He was going to school then, getting his doctorate and he was also working. But his hours were not so long and drawn out and he would spend weekends with him because I would be at the hospital. And he was taking care of him and the apartment and everything else, so that we certainly had competent help, from both the babysitter and from my husband.

Q: You never had any feelings of emotional conflict with this babysitter?

A: No, I've always done one thing. When we moved to the country which was just about a month and a half or two months before the second child was born, we hired a neighbor, a friend and neighbor to take care of the children. She has taken care of them now for 14 years, the same woman. So that the three of them have known no one else but her as far as a mother substitute is concerned. And what I've always done is this: the person who takes care of the children goes home when I come home so that I then have the kids to myself, there isn't any conflict in that. The person that takes care of the house, the cleaning, the cooking, etc. is the one who sleeps in and she is not responsible for the children unless we should go out and she babysits. I wanted it that way because I was terribly jealous, a very jealous mother. I couldn't stand to have a person to take care of the kids with me around.

Q: But you were able to do that by dividing those functions in the household.

A: Yes, except for the first child and the first three years of his life.

Q: Why do you work?

A: I enjoy working and I do not enjoy all day long child care and housewifely activities. I enjoy cooking a gourmet meal now and then, and I love being home with the kids in the summer, even all day. But I like to work. I like to feel I'm contributing something to society, more than just raising children. Yet I think it is the hardest thing in the world to be a good mother. It is easy to be a pediatrician; you train and this is something specific. It is more difficult to be a good parent, in general.

Q: Do you feel that your children have accepted your working? How do they feel about it?

A: I've thought about it sometimes. I've wondered, of course. As the children get older their problems get bigger. I think it is interesting that both the boys have said that their wives will stay home. I don't know whether this is just a teenage thing or if this will actually happen or not. But right now my teenage boys tell me that their wives are going to do what they tell them, and that they are going to stay home and take care of the kids.

When I had the option of going back to work full-time, four years ago now, we discussed it with the family. I asked them what they thought of it, whether it was a good idea or not and they said, "Yes, why don't you try

it? It is an opportunity for you, sort of an advancement."
And so I did. And they didn't complain, they really
haven't outwardly complained. They seemed to do well
I think. I don't notice that they are any worse or un-
happier, worse in behaving, etc. or unhappier than when
I worked part-time.

Q: Do you think they're proud of your position?

A: Yes, I think in many ways they are.

Q: How about your girls? Supposedly a working
mother is good for the girls.

A: Yes, right. I think that's true because they have
ambitions to be mothers, teachers, and doctors.

Q: They want to be several things and they feel it
works out.

A: Yes.

Q: Then you had the complete support of your husband
all the way?

A: Oh, yes, even encouragement I would say, not just
support but encouragement.

Q: And when you became discouraged?

A: Yes, at times when I've been very guilt stricken, that
this was not the right thing to do, when small problems
came up and I immediately attributed them to the fact
that I wasn't here and I should have been, he always reas-
sures me that it couldn't possibly be so. In the present
position, I'm one of the senior members of the staff in my
department and I need to contribute more to the literature; and I don't find the time to do it. But he keeps
encouraging me, "Take several hours in the library and
bone up, do the research, and get your papers written."
But I'm bogged down on that, I never get a chance. I don't
feel I have the time to devote to that.

Q: Do you feel that there is some sacrifice in your
professional career because of the double role?

A: I think it's both. One of the things I have discovered,

I think, is with a career you can get by in both; you can be an adequate physician, or whatever you choose to do, you can be an adequate parent, wife, homemaker, etc., but I don't think you can be the best in each and that bothers me, because I would like to do my very best in both. You also tread a very tight rope. I'm sure you know this. My oldest son was injured playing football two years ago and spent most of the fall in the hospital. He had four hospitalizations and my whole system just fell apart. There is no room for anything like this. Something goes wrong and you're sunk. And I termed that year a year of pain and defeat. I decided then that it was not really possible to be a first-class career woman and a first-class parent, wife, homemaker. That was the first time actually it really hit me. I think my age also has something to do with it. I'm getting tired, I'm 44 now. I don't have as much stamina as I used to. I was never afraid of anything. I had lots of energy.

Q: That's what I would like to know. You felt that you were physically energetic, that you could go without sleep?

A: Oh, yes. Right. I could do anything. It wasn't until the fourth one came along that I began to think, well I really couldn't do this night work with a baby again. By that time I was 36. It was beginning to show then and my husband definitely said he couldn't do any more night work. That was the first time I began to feel a little of that, but it disappeared pretty soon, only I didn't look forward to doing it again. I knew I couldn't really. Then gradually, when I was 42 or so it's shown. I just don't have the physical energy and that's what you need to do this work.

Q: You say your first doubts came when they were teenagers. Do you feel that the older children take more than the younger as far as the parent is concerned?

A: Little children have little problems, easily solved.

Somebody takes their toy, some little thing like that. With older children, there are problems involving basic values, ideals, matters of school work, which become more important, interpersonal relationships, much more difficult.

Q: Do you think that in order to provide the proper supervision you have to give up something? What kinds of things do you have to cut out? Do you have to give up social life?

A: You're too tired for social life! Yes, social life has certainly been cut down. We made it an unwritten rule within our family that we as parents would not go out, for instance, more than one weekend night. Otherwise, we find during the winter that every single weekend we would have social engagements. We went to the theater, someone's house for dinner, sometimes it would be two nights and we just had to cut it out. Not both Friday and Saturday nights. We had to do that and reserve Sunday for the family.

Q: And you are able to have a very warm family life in this time?

A: Yes, when children have a definite structure and they know that Sunday is going to be the day for everybody. We don't always go off and do something. The boys may go down and play football or baseball or something. We're all here. We all have dinner together. That sort of thing. With the boys and I think with the girls, during the four years when I was in practice, I used to set an afternoon aside for each one, just that child and me to do whatever they wanted to do. We ended up walking in the woods most of the time.

Q: But they were alone with you and they felt that this was their special time.

A: Yes, that worked nicely. Then, we also, either Friday or Saturday night that we didn't go out, we would hold game night and each child would have a chance to choose a game to be played and all the family would play. And that was very pleasant and we enjoyed that.

Q: Did any of the literature or writings on women and so forth ever effect you along the way, or did you or your basic ideals and your husband's support give you direction?

A: No, only to the point that when we would meet a woman accomplishing something we would applaud it. I don't think we were ever deterred by any negative report about the failure of women in public life who tried to combine careers, but we certainly applauded the successes.

Q: Then you think your husband's interest in psychology kept him from any particular popularization of family roles?

A: Yes, I think so, of having to assert his masculinity and be the driving force. I think so. He's an extremely reasonable man. I've never known anybody who had more ability to be reasonable. Anybody who had troubles—he used to be in private practice too—he'd say "Go to work" to the woman. Very helpful.

Q: He felt that work would make them feel useful?

A: Yes, it gave women outside interests and a sense of accomplishing something—getting away from the drudgery and just being tied down to being a cook, nurse, cleaner.

Q: A sense of yourself?

A: Yes.

Q: We've covered a lot. What do you think society should do to encourage women and help those who wish to combine work and family?

A: That's a most difficult question, because it's an age-old one. I think it's a matter of male supremacy. Once we solve this problem, which is probably never going to be solved, because the men will not allow it to be. I mean most men will not allow it to be solved. It is as simple as that. Even if you agree that women should work, agreement has to be made about how to share the family chores, etc. I think it is perfectly fine to be again assigned the usual feminine role and it doesn't really bother me. But women cannot solve their problems alone.

Q: What are your feelings about day care?

A: Good day care is very good, but I don't think this changes the man's attitude. Most men secretly feel that their wives should be there at home, even while they are away. Another problem is that the husband's career is also demanding. My husband's career was also soaring and at a peak and he was away a great deal. Once careers go up, you can't go down again. You like the work and the prestige. You build up to be somebody and who wants to go down the totem pole? More and more responsibilities are put on you.

Q: So you found managing two successful careers complicated?

A: Yes. I have given up many things such as traveling or going to meetings as one of the prices you pay.

Q: Do you think there is more prejudice against women in medicine?

A: Well, medical schools are a man's world; and many men will tell you that in no uncertain words. However, if you make it through medical school, pediatrics is a good field for women. You might have more trouble trying to go into surgery. Psychiatry without night work is also easier for a woman and several hospitals have arranged training programs taking the needs of mothers into account. Group practice, of course, is a boon to both men and women.

Q: Then in your field of pediatrics you have found little prejudice?

A: One of the things men resent in any career is absenteeism in women because of their children being sick. "Oh, she's unreliable. Her child is sick, she won't be in for the next two or three days." Many women lose a lot of time from work, and men resent it . . . it's not right of them but they do.

I was determined this wouldn't happen to me. I went to work, did my best, and kept my family problems separate. I never missed a day from work. My babysitter, who has been absolutely marvelous, has never missed a day for 14 years. I could not have done it without my friend. She loves children and enjoys this kind of work. If my children are sick, I diagnose them and can leave them in her care without worry. Only when my son was in the hospital, I could not be with him and be at work at the same time.

Q: If you were giving some young women advice from your own experience, what would you say?

A: Get your training when your children are very young and then work part-time until your children are really grown up—maybe even out of the home and in high school and college. The children can be successful, happy, well-adjusted—as I think mine are—but it's just too fatiguing. For myself it's a matter of my own fatigue.

Q: Yet you would continue to work?

A: Yes, I think I'm really a better mother because I work. I'm happy to see them when I come home. It's very nice to come home and be greeted with four different stories at once. When I don't work, I'm with the family. I'm committed to work and I'm committed to the family.

17

NANCY McCORMICK RAMBUSCH

Not Merely
Husband's Wife or
Children's Mother

*Nancy McCormick Rambusch is presently an
executive and educational consultant with Responsive
Environments Corporation. Previously she has been
founder and headmistress of Whitby School in Green-
wich, Connecticut, and president of the American Montessori Society. She is completing her Ph.D. at Columbia
in French literature, writes frequently for publication
and lectures widely. Her children are twelve and fifteen.
She is an example of a working woman who has been
continuously committed to a professional career.*

There is nothing dramatic in my being a 40-year-old
professional woman with children, living in a marriage
which is a partnership, except that as a practicing Roman
Catholic, the odds against such an arrangement are
enormous.

I have "known" since childhood that married women

who work and do not have to are working for luxuries
and not necessities. They are restricting their families in
the desire for wordly success and/or greater personal
freedom. They are in danger not only of losing their
souls and their husband's and children's esteem, but that
sticky residue of ill-defined, if fervently believed in,
femininity as well—femininity which is the glory of the
Blessed Mother and the bane of Lucifer. Such women are
not corresponding to their true natures and are stifling
their maternal gifts. Such women are committing un-
natural acts, for what else can willful work "outside the
home" be called?

How have I come to ignore the tribal certainties of
my Holy Angels Academy days? What wakened me from
that dream so aptly codified by the Christian Family
Movement as categorical submission to husbandly and
episcopal authority? Why have I eschewed my role as
"heart" of the home to my husband's "head," as Jane to
his Tarzan, as socket to his plug? How could I leave my
children to do the "world's" work when my woman's
work was being neglected? My education and my experience are to blame for my present state. The roots of a
"democratic alternative" to Christian marriage go back
to my childhood.

I grew up in an expansive but unorthodox Irish
family, the youngest of five daughters. My mother had a
master's degree from the University of Wisconsin and
taught English in the college she had attended, before
her marriage. After marriage, she no longer "worked."
Instead, she bore five children in seven years. Despite the
very real constraints of rearing closely spaced children,
my mother viewed with considerable skepticism the then
and now prevalent notion that wives and husbands were
yoked like oxen for eternity. Nor were mother and

children yoked until the youngest child had attained his majority and fled the familial nest. My mother was an independent and private person who never defined herself simply as her husband's wife or her children's mother. The ferocity with which she clung to a definition of herself separable from her conjugal and maternal functions was something of a novelty in our pleasantly pious childhood world.

My mother, however, was plagued by the contradiction between an education which ought to have "led" to something other than diffuse transmission of cultural values, and the possession of reproductive organs which she was mandated to keep operational at all times. Her world defined woman as either consecrated virgin or mother and it was difficult to see what an educated woman, not a nun, might "do," once married, that was not in violation of the sacred canons of motherhood. My own mother's mother came to Cleveland in the 1880s from County Mayo and entered the household of the Mark Hannas as a seamstress. Soon after, she married a captain of a Great Lakes freighter and moved to Milwaukee to rear a three-child family, limited no doubt by her husband's prolonged absences. The eldest son went to the Seminary, my mother and the younger son, to college. My grandmother was committed to the best for my mother and when she married an aspiring young doctor, could only have been pleased.

Indeed, my mother's dilemma derived not from her marriage or the demands of child rearing, but from the burden of gentility and social practice which forbade her using her considerable talents in a professional way, or indeed satisfying way, or in thinking that she could not so use them. Her philanthropies were diocesan, her horizons parochial, not because she wished them so, but be-

cause social service through the Church meant the inevitable mediation of her projects by curates notable for
modesty of intellect and good nature where "ladies'
groups" were concerned.

As my sisters and I grew up and the catechetical certainties of childhood receded, the second world war and
its aftermath posed unprecedented problems for young
Catholic women. My older sisters were putting their
husbands through school. The old patterns of Catholic
marriage were eroding rapidly and those who perceived
an alternative to them had a unique chance to strike out
in new directions. I was one who struck out. I recall
spirited discussions with classmates in Paris in which we
speculated on the validity of exchanging known intellectual joys for the possibly illusory joys of little feet. A
group of us vowed never to marry but we soon weakened,
when we saw the possibility of combining a life of the
spirit with one of the ovaries. Forgive our retrospective
dualism; only later did we come to see life in more inte-
grated terms. I suspect that like our mothers, we too
accepted unconsciously the virgin/mother polarity and
could think of no adequate way to situate ourselves in
life as spinsters.

My marriage was particularly auspicious for the development of new directions. My husband was an artist
and remarkably free of pious preconceptions about conjugal and family life. We lived in New York, and I
started graduate school, pregnant, as soon as we were
settled. Our first child was born in the middle of exams
and the contrapuntal world of school and marriage was
one we accommodated ourselves to with pleasure. I went
pregnant (with a two-year-old in tow) to England for a
year of study, leaving my husband behind. My father
loaned us the money for me to go. My husband visited

me when he could. In the early 1920s my father, then a young doctor, had gone to Vienna to study for a year, leaving his wife and two small children behind. No doubt in the early 1980s my daughter Alexandra may well go abroad to study for a year leaving both husband and small children behind.

As a result of my year in England, I became the matrix of a small but pithy social movement which made even greater and more unorthodox demands on my time and family life than had the time been spent abroad. The demands continued, though transformed into teaching positions or present managerial ones. Why do I work? I work for the same reason my mother worked, though she had difficulty accomplishing much that was satisfying to her personally beyond the rearing of five children, a not inconsiderable accomplishment. I work because I am not merely my husband's wife or my children's mother. I had ambitions for self-realization which preceded my marriage and parallel it. I never conceived of marriage as the sole mechanism for self-realization. Working has not been for me an alternative to "staying at home."

Like many other similarly educated couples (though not necessarily Catholic ones) my husband and I combined marriage and careers from the outset. I have yet to discover compelling reasons outside disincarnated Catholic rhetoric why I should not work, or alternately why I should stay at home. I cannot compare the life I might have had with the one I do have, since the evolution of that life to its present form was gradual and almost imperceptible. Each opportunity to work at something new presented itself to me, at the time as a special case; each decision I made committed me further professionally.

It is not irrelevant that I have two, not eight children,

a fact which accounts in part for my "early admission" to the working world. Perhaps it is a mark of my "contemporarity," perhaps of my hardness of heart, that I feel now as I did at the time and spacing of their emergence, not at all apologetic for so few. Family limitation within an orthodox Catholic framework focused on rhythm, field hockey, and abstinence for my generation of young marrieds, but that did not preclude our making a conscious decision in favor of a small family.

Now my children, a son and a daughter, are respectively 15 and 12. When they were very young, my principal concern was to find a competent surrogate mother for them in the periods of my absence. I was fortunate in the grandmotherly French woman who cared for the children for the four years dating from my daughter's birth. She did no other child minding, and so was always available either to come to our home or have the children brought to hers. The logistics of child care are enormously complicated for working mothers, particularly since the mothers are generally expected (or were, in my time) to function socially at all levels of stereotypical feminine competence as though they never left the house. Getting oneself and one's small children organized at dawn before leaving for work, sandwiching in shopping en route home, managing upsets in routine, all demand prodigies of anticipatory design. Unfortunately, in my early working days there were few, if any, adequate day-care facilities for the children of young professional women—and there are still few. The arrangements for adequate child care are certainly the most difficult single problem for women leaving home.

I have never consulted my children about the "shape" of my husband's and my common life. Recently I was asked about my children's reactions to the notion of our moving back to New York after having lived several years in Connecticut. We never asked our children to respond to the idea of our moving; we simply moved. My husband's and my work were in New York; usually, there is less emphasis on a child-centered family existence when both parents work. To partisans of home-with-mother, this apparent lack of constant concern for children's every reaction may appear heartless. But adult-oriented families offer children other kinds of experiences. There are not two clear-cut generations in our family, despite our occasional autocratic decision-making. The enduring closeness that I, as one of five, found with my sister Monica, but not my mother, my daughter may well find with me.

Of course, the American popular literature of the '50s, my initiatory decade of child rearing, glorified the large family mediated by mother as domestic engineer. My own inclination and competence dictated a move in the opposite direction. At present, the pendulum is swinging to a more general acceptance of women with young children working for pleasure as well as profit. Young people are delineating gender roles far less clearly than did we. (Marshall McLuhan assures us that genital sexuality is on the way out; Pope Paul, on the other hand, hopes that it is on the way back in.) A backward glance at the notion of the family in the Christian West proves that the closely knit interpersonally involved nuclear version of it does not pre-date industrialization. Peter Laslett and Phillipe Aries assure us that the very notion of childhood is of recent origin, as is the notion of a motherhood with an all-embracing concern for exclusivity in child rearing. Women's departure from motherhood thus recently defined indicates no heinous familial or female rejection of transcendent values. I am relieved to know that the family life I enjoy is not the penultimate expression of social disaster, as I was assured repeatedly it would be during school days at St. Roberts School in Shosewood, Wisconsin (amidst intermittent prayers for the victory of Generalissimo Franco).

My professional life had dealt principally with the education of other mothers' young children. I once thought it a particularly appropriate kind of work for women, but now believe it seemed so because it posed far fewer problems than other occupational interests might have done. Young married women should be able to pursue any interest without the need to justify it on grounds other than personal choice and satisfaction. It is deceitful to mollify critics of working women by promoting the notion that nursing, teaching, and social work are justifiable for women mainly because they represent "mothering" activities. Many of the young women with whom I work, teachers, single and recently married, have decided to combine marriage and work, perceiving a relationship between the two, much as I did a decade and a half ago. They are not asking their fiance's or husband's permission to work, or for a definition of their duties, once married; rather, they are discussing their ambitions well in advance of the ceremony. The pooling of ambitions and resources is a common experience among the educated young.

Married middle class ladies now in their mid-forties to mid-fifties with almost grown children are reentering the working world in prodigious numbers, or are entering it for the first time. Their earning power is generally minuscule compared to their husband's, hence poses no problem. The change in their definition of themselves as wife and mother and their family's willingness to subscribe to such a change looms larger. To most employers, women are thought of as childless widows. Working women have to think of themselves, at least during working hours, in this way. For some of my contemporaries this abdication of what they have come to believe themselves to be by both nature and clerical mandate, asks too much. But it will not be too hard for many of my young friends in 30 years' time. Child rearing and "working" are not necessarily competitive activities if one does not elect to make them so. Women who want to work will be able to do so far more easily in the future than they have in the past. Here's to the future where the working mother will be at least as normative as the stay-at-home mother has been.

18

AGNES BROWN

I Wanted to Get Off Welfare; Work Means You're Doing Something

Agnes Brown is the pseudonym of a divorced black mother with five sons, three in their early twenties, one an old teenager, and one still in elementary school. She has had to work most of her life; for many years she has been the head of her household. She went back to business school on scholarship and by getting a better job was able to get off welfare. She speaks eloquently of the freedom, enjoyment and self-respect which her work provides. She now does some teaching and is a secretary for her church.

Q: [1] What is your name?
A: Agnes Brown.

[1] This account of the experience of combining work and child rearing was written from a personal interview. Both the interviews and the essays in this book derived from the questionnaire which appears in the Appendix.

Q: How did you get involved in your work here in the church?

A: Well, my children became involved by starting to come to Sunday school. Some of their friends were coming here to Sunday school. The children were so excited and all so I just started out being a Sunday school helper around the class and eventually I started becoming more and more involved. I've been doing Sunday school work for a long time. I took time out to have my last son, in 1958, and then came back again.

Q: What kind of work do you do now?

A: I now work as a full-time secretary and registration worker. In the job definition it is called assistant programmer, but it is the same kind of thing—a girl Friday who answers the phone and does the letters.

Q: Every day?

A: Yes. And during this past fall I had also to do the choir playing with one hand.

Q: What kind of jobs have you had before?

A: When I first graduated from high school I worked in a factory. It was very discouraging because I had an academic diploma, but I couldn't get the job I wanted to. There were several office openings but I couldn't get them.

Q: Do you think this was directly related to discrimination against Negroes?

A: Yes, because I knew that I could type better than the girl they hired, but I couldn't say anything. I really didn't want to go into domestic work. After all, I had gone through high school and I had an academic diploma and I wasn't going to do domestic work if I could help it.

Q: So you were working in a factory, what kind of factory?

A: Shirts, and I went from there to another factory—a beer factory. And after that, I got married and didn't go to work for a long time. Finally things got very tight and I had to do a couple of days work here and there. So there I was doing domestic work anyway, since I had to help supplement the family income.

Q: Did you come from a family in which the mother worked? What was your family situation?

A: My mother and my stepfather both worked during the war. I had to help with the chores. I did most of the cooking. There were four of us girls.

Q: Were you the oldest?

A: No, I'm the second youngest of the four. We had a pretty good family relationship actually. During the depression things were very bad, but we were well fed. We didn't really have any family problems on the whole. My mother stayed home, she only got this job during war time in the '40s. You know, it was something to do and they needed it. She wanted to supplement my stepfather's income. Since then she has always done domestic work too.

Q: So there was no feeling in your home that it wasn't right for a woman to work? Do you remember your feelings about that as you grew up?

A: I think all of us children were very much taught to finish high school and go to work. Mainly because we knew how hard it was for our parents to have to struggle and put us through school all those years. Jobs being what they were, pay being so low and all, we weren't a rich family. As a matter of fact we had very little. We girls had to make over the clothes we had. Of course, it was something special when we got something new—wearing so many of my sisters' hand-me-downs for so long. Of course, she got the hand-me-downs too. But we really didn't care much about it. We were born in the country, we were born in Connecticut and we didn't really worry too much. I was just as happy to wear dungarees and sneakers anyway. I was very much of a tomboy. When I finished high school I received a scholarship to go to Hunter College. Dumb me, I didn't want to go.

Q: Do you remember why you didn't want to go?

A: I wanted to get married. I was madly in love at that time. In my last year of high school I was going very steady with my husband, at that time my boyfriend. And I wanted to get married. I wanted to get married and have a beautiful home. I didn't want any children. I just felt that little babies are the worst things in the world. Whenever any of my friends got married and they had a family and they wanted to show me their babies, I wasn't the least bit interested. I didn't care about babies at all.

Q: But you didn't want to work in order to have a career?

A: No. It's funny. I wanted to get married so I could have a beautiful home and I didn't want any children. I don't know what actually was behind all that, except that during our stay at home we had second-hand furniture and everything and we had to clean it, we had to scrub it, and polish it and all that. I guess deep down girls are always looking forward to a home of their own that they can make beautiful and all that.

Q: So you didn't go to college and went to the factory.

A: My mother was heartbroken and now that I look back on it I can really understand how she felt; but I also felt that I should get out of school and work to help out. Believe it or not I only made ten dollars a week at that factory! Half of that would go for car fare because I would go to work in New Jersey and I was living in Staten Island.

Q: But you were planning to get married, right?

A: Yes. I was looking forward to it much more than my husband I'm sure. He wasn't ready for marriage yet.

Q: What was he doing?

A: His background was different from mine. He was a foster child. Had lost his mother when he was only seven and his father had been away from the family for years. So he had it very, very difficult. He had to work nights and try to go to school in the days and he'd be sleeping in the classrooms. He just couldn't make it and finally he had to drop out of school when he was in seventh grade and he had to work because his foster mother expected him to. His was a much more serious problem than mine.

Q: If he was going to get married wouldn't that end his schooling?

A: He wasn't planning to get married. I was planning to get married. You know how girls are. They always think about marriage. He wasn't ready to get married. He got drafted. After he was away he came back to see me and I convinced him to get married, but then it didn't happen for a long time after that either, because his stepmother, or foster mother, had such a terrific hold on him. Now that I look back on it, it was good because he needed someone. He had all sorts of inside problems that developed later.

Q: Did he go into the army?

A: Yes, he went into the army.

Q: And you went to the factory?

A: Yes.

Q: Then what?

A: He came back. I had two children before he got out of the army. I was living with my mother while he was in service and when he came back he wanted to move into his foster mother's home. Much to my regret and objections we did move.

Q: Did you work when you had those two little children in the beginning?

A: No, in the beginning I didn't because I was living

with my mother. I was getting 80 dollars a month and it was enough to carry me and pay my mother room and board.

Q: Did you feel that it was good for the children to have you at home?

A: Right. At that time things were much more reasonable, 25 years ago, than they are now. It wasn't difficult then. I didn't have very many wants, just enough to keep the baby going.

Q: After your husband returned home he got a job?

A: Yes. He had many readjustments to civilian life. Then I began to realize just how much he was immature in his ways. He wasn't ready for a family and fatherhood at all. It was much easier for him when he was in service because I had lived with my mother and then I stayed with his foster mother and that's when everything really got very strained.

Q: Was he able to get a job with a 7th grade education?

A: Yes, he was working in hospitals. From one to another. It became increasingly difficult to manage because he got so involved with so many other things, especially women. As I said, he wasn't ready to settle down. It was very difficult for him. I was silly enough to have more children.

Q: You had no idea of birth control or family planning? You just wanted children?

A: I didn't have as much grit or ambition for family planning as I should have. I tried to instill in him that we should, and he thought it wasn't necessary to do anything.

Q: But you didn't have any religious feelings against birth control.

A: No. I went to a Baptist Sunday school but I didn't keep it up long enough to have any deep religious feelings. I just went because I liked to sing. I had two more children and it was very difficult to stay in my mother-in-law's house. We had only one room there, all six of us in one room. There was no central heating or any hot water or anything. We had a cold stove and had to heat water to take a bath and bathe the children and wash the clothes. Real country. I finally put an application in to the project to get out of there. The only apartments that were big enough for our family size were over here. They had three and four room apartments in Staten Island but we needed five rooms because we had four boys. When the notice came through that we had been accepted for a five-room apartment, it was in New York, my husband didn't want to come. He wanted to stay there because we had a close family, aunts and a foster mother who was elderly and owned this big house. There were many roomers. He was keeping company with one of the roomers who lived on the next floor, as a matter of fact. He'd come home from work, and change and get dressed and he'd be gone. There I am with four boys.

Q: So he wasn't really providing much for the boys.

A: No, through all these years. Now the boys at their ages resent him very much, because he never has been a very strong family figure. But he had had no strong family picture of his own to start off with.

Q: Yes, to begin with.

A: His father was away and he didn't know where. He found out when he was 30 years old. After all those years he thought his father had just left his mother and his father had been in an institution. It was a bitter blow for him to find that out.

Q: At least it meant that his father hadn't deserted. Could he pick up a relationship after that?

A: Yes. He found out that his father was living here in New York City and during the later years of his father's life they were always together.

Q: Maybe he'll have a better relationship with the boys in later years.

A: Well, unfortunately, the boys know the whereabouts of their father now because this woman he lives with is two doors down and she has three children and he's always there. They meet him in the street coming and going all the time, and they have had several hot discussions with him.

Q: This woman has three children?

A: Yes she has three children from him.

Q: And you have five?

A: I'm used to it now. I put up with it for nine years— nine years in June. My little Johnny was just eight months old when the court finally decided to see things my way. I had taken him three times to court. I had finally gotten my eyes open to this whole life ahead of me and I just couldn't see spending the rest of my life being tied to this man who wasn't supporting his children and wasn't presenting any strong male image for his children. He was coming and going.

Q: Did he resent your going to work? When did you resume going to work?

A: During these years I was doing day's work—domestic work—to help out.

Q: That's while you were living at your mother-in-law's?

A: No, I couldn't leave. The boys were all small then. It was a full-time job raising four boys as they were very close together. In between the third and fourth boy I did do a little work. There was two years difference between them and my mother-in-law would keep them or I'd get my mother who was right down the street from me then. But it was very very difficult because it was just *too much* to go out and come back and try to get things going and he was just never any help even on his days off. Never. Right now we have a family crisis because one of my boys

was in jail. That's why I was late this morning. I had to
go see this doctor. I had to go see my son's psychiatrist.
He's under care and he's 23 so I couldn't get any information at all because he is over age. My husband has come to
see me to find out how I made out. He doesn't go and do
all these things. I have to go and take care of everything.

Q: Do you think Negro women have been forced to be
stronger than their men.

A: I have always said that. Of course, it has a lot to do
with your make-up too, but I'm sure a woman, a Negro
woman feels much more capable of getting a job and holding a job than a Negro man does. A man is not willing to
take a job that doesn't pay enough money. He doesn't
have the education or the background to get a better paying job without further training, really. They are just held
down. They have so much pride that they don't think they
need further training. They won't pick themselves up. I
was willing to take any kind of job in order to feed my
children, any legal job.

Q: When did you make up your mind to return to
work?

A: When we moved in 1950 over here. He came because
I was determined to come. We came over here and we had
lots of expenses. He had been sick and he had had an ap-
pendectomy and so we got on emergency welfare until
he could go back to work. The children were little, so we
moved into this apartment and he got a job working as a
parking lot attendant which really wasn't very much, but
it helped a little. We made out, but I finally got to the
stage where I thought I had to go to work because the
children were getting bigger and buying four or five
pairs of shoes at one time was no joke. After my youngest
became five, we decided to put him into nursery school so
I could work full-time. The year before or six months
before I had an operation. I had to have my ovary re-

moved and the doctor told me, "Don't do any heavy work." What are you going to do when you've got children. So I went to work anyway in a hospital and I worked full-time and he was working full-time in a hospital in Staten Island. But he was wasting his money; that's why we were so much in debt.

Q: Who took care of your children at that time?

A: I worked during the daytime and three of them were in school and the other was in nursery school. I worked from 6:30 to 2:00. By the time they got home from school I was home.

Q: Yes.

A: The minute I started working he started to bring home less and less money from work. He went and bought himself a car.

Q: Do you think he was unhappy with your working?

A: He was glad because it gave him more freedom to throw his money away. We went into this thing with our eyes open hoping that we could get more bills paid off, and make a go of it. It didn't work out that way because he got very easily diverted to cars and women and gambling. I gave up the job after one year because I needed to stay home with the kids. They were getting into difficulties in school because of the problems in the home.

Q: What kind of signs did you feel in them that made you quit work?

A: Well, with the second son, whom I'm having trouble with now, he never was one to talk very much and he would stay in the street late at night when he was only eight or nine. When we wanted to know why he did such a thing, he couldn't tell us. I suppose it was because of the difficulty with his father, he and I were having fights and so forth. He felt it more than the rest of the boys, I guess.

Q: Would they cry when you went to work?

A: No. They were all in school. The youngest one was the bother at that time and he went to nursery school. He adjusted to that.

Q: Did nursery school take all your money from your job?

A: No. It was very nice. It only cost me $1.50 a week.

Q: Was it some kind of public cooperative thing?

A: Yes. It was one of these projects. The projects have a nursery program, day care, and they only charge $1.50. I only worked a year because he was going through money and I thought it was foolish for me to just throw his away. So I stopped work. And by George we nearly starved. I lost 20 pounds after that. He had gotten so used to his habits that he couldn't revert. So we struggled on for a year. I got discouraged.

Q: Were you on welfare at any time?

A: I think we did get on welfare again. Not at that point, but soon after that, because he went from one job to another and he couldn't make it and was laid off for a while and then got another job. We got on welfare when he got laid off. When he did get another job we didn't get off welfare because he didn't want to. The welfare check was coming in my name.

Q: Yes.

A: Then he got himself a job and then we moved out of those houses.

Q: This was getting near the end?

A: Yes. We went through lots of years and he had this woman and that woman until finally I got to the stage where I just didn't care any more. I was just going to raise my children. So in 1962 I took this business course.

Q: How did you get the money for that?

A: A scholarship from the church, the parish had scholarships where they would further the education of anyone who needed it. It was very beneficial for me. I had long talks with the boys and I told them that I could get off of welfare and go to work if they would all just stay in school and finish. Because they always felt very embarrassed by being on welfare and the other children would tease them about it. I was willing to go to work but they must stay in school. Which didn't work out, because not one of them got a diploma, all four of the kids dropped out of school.

Q: That must have been really heartbreaking.

A: It was, because they all have such potential. All over 100 I.Q.s, every one of them. Fortunately, two of them have gone back to school and one of them is doing very well. One of them is doing very well in a book publishing firm downtown. This is the one who is 21.

Q: He went back to night school?

A: Yes, he worked and went to night school.

Q: This was something that he did?

A: Yes, each child wanted to get on his feet and make something of himself. Just to show the world that they can. It was very difficult because even though they had me, there was also their father, who never made it. He's still struggling now. I don't know what kind of work he is doing now. He has a psychiatric problem which comes and goes. I had to go to work so that the children could have one steady kind of parent.

Q: Well, when you went back to the business course did you find it difficult to go back to school?

A: No, I loved it. I thought it was just great. I really loved it. I took a refresher course in typing. I learned Gregg shorthand and bookkeeping. I was just sorry it was over in six months. During that time I was on welfare which was good because I had the organization here get in touch with them and tell them that they were giving me a scholarship but it was only for schooling and it was not to support my family. So they kept on supporting me until I got finished and went to work full-time myself. And the only thing that happened to me since then was that there was a change in my husband's attitude; he even tried to get a job. And he came back. That's when I had this last child, which was so stupid on my part, although, of course, I'm glad for it now. He had been on the outs with his last girlfriend and staying home very regularly and I thought maybe we could turn over a new leaf and I was amazed when he said he was going to really try to make it.

Q: What about the pregnancy?

A: It was a shock to me after ten years.

Q: Yes.

A: And then I found out a month later that his girlfriend also was pregnant. I went flying up to a legal agency and filed divorce proceedings or something. They told me that I couldn't because they said something about ignorance of the law is no excuse, or something or other.

Q: Did you find that after you started having babies you liked them? At the beginning, you said that you hadn't wanted babies?

A: Yes, oh yes. It was really a great joy actually, and later in life I realized that was the only joy I got out of the whole marriage. Even with all their problems of getting colds and pneumonia and scratched knees and no food and ragged clothes and things. Just to watch them grow. Hopefully they'll all become solid citizens. I think they'll make it. I'm not sure. I'm praying.

Q: It is a struggle.

A: At least one or two of them will and you can't expect miracles.

Q: Do you think the whole black revolution and the

whole stirring Negro community have made it different for your life and perhaps a better life for you and your children?

A: I don't think it's made a difference in my life so much, because I've never known real discrimination because I had been born and raised in Connecticut. When I first came to Staten Island I was nine and it was at that time when I fully realized it—I was different from other children. Up until then I hadn't, because it was a small community and we had been accepted by everyone in the community. We have Indian ancestors, my uncle is much more Indian than I am. It was very difficult at first, when I first came. I first knew myself as colored. I never let it bother me. I went to a predominantly white school in elementary school and high school.

Q: So it was just when you began to work and saw job discrimination?

A: Then it didn't bother me too much. Even now, I'm the type of person that doesn't let things bother them for too long because life is too short and there are many more important things to do.

Q: What do you feel that your work gives you now? Why do you work?

A: I enjoy it. I *Enjoy* it. The secretarial work is very important because I realize that I'm a great help to the boss. I enjoy being able to help them and find things that they can't find and do things for them to help them. It relieves them for an opportunity to do other things and of course I especially enjoy working with children. It's so gratifying. I always try to stay with younger children. For a couple years I had older classes and they taught me more than I taught them, but it was great. You get to feel so free to do so many things. Not so much for them or for yourself as with them.

Q: Then the financial aspect is just a part of it?

A: Yes. I first started out I was only making $62.00 a week and I had a very difficult time getting off welfare, believe it or not. They didn't believe that I was making enough money to support my family. So, I had to get the bookkeeper to send them over a letter and say how much I was making and that I wanted to get off welfare. They sent me a check anyway and I had to send it back.

Q: You thought that was important for your children?

A: Yes, it made them feel much more free too. But due to the environment that we lived in and the neighborhood, they were so discouraged with the school system. The school system in New York is ridiculous, absolutely ridiculous. Of course, they have improved a lot in the last couple of years, but the only way that could be of an advantage to my boys is if they went back to night school.

Q: How do you think your youngest boy, now, responds to your work?

A: He brags about it. I'm sure it's because he's young yet. One of them, the one who is 19, I'm sure he resents my working. He thinks I spend entirely too much time with the church, but if I didn't he wouldn't eat. I have not put very many restrictions on my boys because when we were living together as a family unit there were lots of restrictions. My husband tried to do this but wasn't able to. So he would end up beating them and striking them. I always thought it was very cruel. Children just don't respond to this.

Q: No.

A: So we just have great conversations I and the boys. Even now that they're grown. But I've always been the kind of mother who tried very hard not to push, to let them feel their way, to see where they think it's best to

live. But, each child is so different. What works for one
doesn't work for the other one, you know. Then you
wonder, "Gosh what'll I try next?" What will work for
this one and what won't work for that one? It's an endless
struggle.

Q: Well, do you see anything that would help working
women generally. Things that have helped you that would
be a good thing if it could be made more general.

A: I don't know. Day care is a godsend for a mother
who has small children, especially when they have to
work. It's much better than a paid babysitter because they
are learning while they are there and they have structured
programs.

Q: The mother gets an extensive report?

A: When they are older—that's the problem when they
get to be too old for day care and go into the public
school. There are now, of course, after-school programs.
But the children don't always attend them unless they
think there is something that is going to be exciting for
them, so the curriculum has to be remade.

Q: It can't be just a babysitter?

A: No, better something to help them with their work.
Which is so important, especially for the Negro community. Not just staying after school to paint benches and
draw a picture. They need something much more stimulating than that.

Q: Yes, much more. What kind of advice would you
give someone beginning now to go to work and starting
a family?

A: I think the main thing would be that if you do have
to work, to sit down and thoroughly discuss it with your
husband, because if you are working and he resents it,
it's a losing battle. If it can be worked out where it is
compatible for both, then it's ideal, for you're both work-

ing for the same goals. Then it will be something that you are looking forward to or working for, be it a new car, a new home or what have you, but you also have to find time for your children. And that I think is very important. I'm grateful that I have boys because I'm very athletic so we would go out and swim, ride bicycles, and do all those kinds of things together. As each one got older they drifted away from doing things with mama, but the main thing is that they all would like to do it with you then.

Q: What about after school? How do you arrange now for the ten-year-old?

A: He goes to school downtown, so he takes two buses, but there is a program which he is involved in that is connected with the camp he goes to and they have a big community house down on 94th Street two blocks from the school. They have after-school sessions there, so he can go for recreation—three days a week he goes. Then one day he goes ice skating with the class. That takes care of four days until 5:30. Most of the time he comes by here and I wait for him. We plan things together for the evenings, if I have to come to choir I bring him—he likes that. We do things together and I plan things together for the weekends, but he has gotten to the stage now that he wants to be with his friends rather than his mother so. . . .

Q: Do you think living in the city has made it more difficult for you?

A: Suburbs are ideal, but you kind of get lost in your own bright little world in the suburbs and you're not really aware of what is going on in other neighborhoods, in other areas, unless you hear it on the news or read the paper. The city is an ideal place for opportunity, but if I really had my way I think I would move out of the city.

Although it's full of opportunities it also has its drawbacks. Even in a big crowded city your next door neighobr could be a total stranger to you, where in a small community you know your next door neighbor, you'd spend time with them. You have them over for cocktails or cards or dinner. In the city everyone is in their own little shell. They're afraid. Fear. One thing that the church has tried to do here in this neighborhood, is to show the community that we care about the people in the community, and join them in their problems by going to court with them and their children, going to school with them, and their parents, even to share in their basketball games. We go to show we are not just four walls.

Q: I think the kind of scholarship that you got to return to school is an excellent idea.

A: It puts people on their own. To show people their worth. It proves to people that they are somebody. Work really gives you a sense of freedom that you've never had before, even when you are getting a welfare check while sitting home. You think, well you've got money coming and you don't have any worries. That's not true, at all. Going to work every day gives you a sense of freedom and it means you're doing something. Not only are you getting money for it, but you're holding a respectable job—like this job. I love this job; it is so gratifying to walk down the street and have children shouting at you and calling you. They remember me from one year to the next. That means so much.

CYNTHIA C. WEDEL

Spending Women's Second Life Creatively

Cynthia Wedel is in her fifties and holds the very demanding post of President of the National Council of Churches. She entered her present career as a professional administrator after twenty years of homemaking, a return to graduate school, some teaching, and many activities as a volunteer in church and civic affairs. She stresses the importance of volunteer experience and a return to study as a preparation for full-time work when the children have left home. She also gives a perspective on the working wife's decisions in the later years of marriage.

My story is not that of the mother of young children who goes to work, but of one returning to full-time employment after the children were grown and away from home. Yet it may include some insights which are useful to others. After all, mine is one of the most typical experiences of modern American women. Like so many others,

after college I took a job—as a director of Christian education. Then came marriage and twenty-five years of full-
time homemaking. I really never considered working after
I was married. Now, in my 50s, I find myself back in the
world of work. I suspect that this will increasingly be the
life pattern of today's women.

Those of us who did not have a keen desire to pursue a
chosen career, and who did not feel the economic necessity to work while bringing up children, were probably
very fortunate. But as I look around at my contemporaries,
I realize how many of us did not look ahead. Homemaking and mothering are so absorbing and time consuming
that it takes considerable imagination to envisage a time
when they will suddenly be drastically lessened. Adjusting
to a new freedom from heavy responsibility takes many
different forms. Some women manage to keep themselves
busy in and around their homes, although this seems to
me rather a poor use of time and talent with the ease of
housekeeping today. As statistics indicate, a rather tragi-
cally large number of women with too much time on their
hands and feeling unneeded, get sick or take to alcohol
or frequent the psychiatrist's couch. Wiser ones—and may
their numbers increase!—move out into the community
and give urgently needed help as volunteers.

Those of us who go to work at this period of our lives
do so for a variety of reasons. Sadly, of course, quite a
large number have to because of their husbands' deaths.
Women still outlive men by a substantial number of years.
Some women who have no economic pressure to work
have said they do it to give a kind of "focus" to their lives.
Without a job, and with greatly diminished household
tasks, they find themselves either drifting aimlessly, or
being pressured almost unbearably to take part in every
volunteer activity and fund-raising campaign in the com-

munity. A number of women have told me that they finally took a job because it was the only way to be respectably unavailable for the increasing demands.

There are probably others like myself who did it, not out of severe economic pressure, but in order to provide a little more adequately for old age. My husband is older than I am, and is a minister. His salary never permitted us to save a great deal and his pension is low and fixed. We had discussed often over the years the idea of my going to work when he retired in order to build up a little "backlog" for complete retirement. This I did, and have been working in a church related administrative job for the past six years.

Out of my experience I have developed a number of convictions which I am eager to share with other women. As I talk with young girls, I want to urge them to get as complete an education as possible before entering into a period of full-time homemaking. It is far easier to finish high school, or college—whichever is a girl's plan—in the normal course of schooling than it is to go back later and finish. I would find it hard to count the number of women whom I have heard bemoaning the fact that they neglected that last year or two of formal education! If this has seemed important to my generation, it will be far more so for the women of tomorrow as educational standards and requirements are constantly being raised. The current custom of marrying during college, or even high school, years will almost surely bring many regrets later in life. If the love for a man is real enough to be a basis for a good marriage, it ought to be real enough to stand a year or two of waiting.

A second conviction which has grown on me since I went back to work is the great value of volunteer activity during the homemaking years. From many points of view it is a good thing for a woman to have interests beyond the home all through those years. Even when the children are very young, it is wise to team up with other mothers and to take turns keeping the children so that each one can have a day or a half day a week to do a volunteer job. It is good for the children not to be totally dependent on you. It gives you a fresh outlook on life. You will even find that you like your children better when you have been away from them for a few hours!

It was my experience that as our two children grew older, they were pleased and proud of my community activities, even when occasionally they had to fend for themselves. It makes you a more interesting person to your children and to your husband when you have some activities to discuss other than purely domestic ones.

I probably should confess here that I took this advice a little too seriously and became almost over-involved in volunteer work. I cannot see now that it did my family any real harm, but there were times when my activities interfered with things I might have done for and with my husband. Another woman's husband might not have been as patient and understanding as mine was.

However, if a woman is going to return to the world of work after her children are grown, active involvement in a part-time job or in volunteer work is extremely important. Homemaking and child rearing, important as they are, do not include many skills that have commercial value. But serious volunteer work can. During my "volunteer" career, I took numerous training courses—in such things as administration, social service skills and public relations. At some periods I did concentrated office work, learned how to operate a switchboard, improved my typing ability, had good experience as a receptionist. At other times my experience consisted of helping to plan and conduct training courses, run conferences and meetings, make speeches and preside. I met professionally trained people from whom I learned many important lessons and who were eager to help when I wanted a job. While one's motives for volunteering may be primarily to be helpful to others, there are a great many surprising "fringe benefits."

Another of my experiences has, I believe, value for other women. About five years before my husband planned to retire, we discussed what kind of a job I might think about. While my volunteer work, and my earlier work in the church offered several possibilities, we both thought teaching might be the best answer. I had gradually drifted into a good deal of volunteer teaching both in church and in various organizations. I liked it and seemed to do well at it. And as we looked ahead, teaching seemed to blend well with continued homemaking, and offered those lovely, long vacations! But all my good volunteer experience was not enough to fulfill the requirements for teaching. Therefore, with my husband's enthusiastic encouragement, I went back to school.

Because I had graduated from college and had a master's degree—by this time very out of date—I decided to try to get a Ph.D. History had been my earlier subject, but now my interest was more in psychology, especially social psychology and group work. I was at that time too deeply involved in some of my volunteer activities—including being national president of United Church Women, which required a great deal of travel—to enroll for full-time study. I found that most universities are a little reluctant to accept middle-aged women as doctoral candidates, for this requires considerable faculty time and attention which needs to go to those who are really serious about their future work.

However, a university in my home city said that I

could start in and take all the psychology courses which I would have needed for an undergraduate major, and for a master's degree. If I completed these satisfactorily, they would then consider whether or not to accept me. It took almost five years to take all these courses—one or two a semester, and a couple in summer school. There were a number of times when I doubted whether I could do it. I had thought of psychology in terms of stimulating courses on abnormal psychology, child psychology, or counseling. The rigors of tough courses in experimental and physiological psychology, the struggle to learn German, and three required courses in statistics were more than I had bargained for! But I realize now that the hard discipline of this required work—competing with keen young students almost thirty years my junior—did me a great deal of good. They made real to me the fact of which I had read, that the ability to learn does not diminish with age. I am by no means a brilliant person, but the motivation and experience which an older person brings to the learning experience can compensate for the lack of quick memorizing ability and the other attributes of youth.

I would not suggest, of course, that every middle-aged woman set out to get a Ph.D. The level of work depends on background, circumstances, and plans for the future. If you haven't finished high school, this would be the goal. If you had two or three years of college, a bachelor's degree may be what is needed. A master's degree is the best credential for many jobs in teaching, social work, guidance. Business training or computer technology may be best for some. The main thing is that returning to school can give new skills, refurbish old ones, and bring one up to date. I would even urge women who have no intention of taking paid employment to do it because the world is changing so fast today that we all need to learn new things about our society and the world in which we live. I only wish now that I had time to take courses in economics, sociology, foreign affairs, and a dozen other of the areas where so much is new.

One of the serious problems of our day is the "generation gap—the difficulty which older people have in understanding the younger generation. Of course, such a gap has always existed. But because of the very rapid rate of change today it seems to be more acute now than in earlier eras. Indeed, if one can take with any seriousness the saying of the teenagers, "You can't trust anyone over thirty," we realize how big a gap exists! A part of this, at least, results from the explosion of knowledge in the past decade or two, and the rapid changes in educational method and content. The more of us of an older generation who can humble ourselves to go back to school with the young, the more possible communication will be between young and old. Those of us who are mothers and grandmothers have a real opportunity to build bridges if we will.

To go back to my own story—after taking all the required courses, I was allowed to become a Ph.D. candidate. This did not require more course work, but a heavy schedule of supervised reading, five days of comprehensive examinations, a dissertation, and a final oral examination. Every step was terrifying—but I'm sure this is true regardless of age. Finally the work was complete and the degree received. At that time, my husband had not as yet retired. It seemed wise to accept a proffered post teaching just one course a semester in a local college. This was a way to get experience in college teaching as well as to keep up my skills.

Then my husband did retire, and soon thereafter I was offered a job in the administration of a national church agency. It was not a teaching job. I am still not at all sure that my having a Ph.D. had anything to do with my getting it. But it seemed wise to accept it at the time. My husband was doing post-retirement teaching in the same city, and the two went well together.

I have been at this now for six years. My husband has kept busy so far with part-time teaching, writing, and lecturing. But I foresee changes ahead. Like all administrative work, mine gets heavier and more demanding all the time. I enjoy it, find it an endless challenge, and feel that I learn something new and valuable almost every day. But it requires more and more work at home, meetings in the evenings and on weekends, and fairly extensive travel. As my husband gets older, a little less robust and less occupied, I face again the wife versus working woman dilemma. It is good to be earning—to be supporting both of us "in the style to which we would like to become accustomed." But the possibilities of the joy of companionship in these later years of our lives is a strong pull toward living more simply, but being together.

This leads to my final insight which I'd like to share with working wives. I have been wonderfully fortunate in the fact that my husband and I have always been able to talk about things even at the level of deep feelings. How seldom do most of us really understand even our own motives, to say nothing of another person's. He knows that I enjoy my work. But he also knows that he matters more to me. I think I am perfectly ready to "dwindle into a wife" (a favorite quotation of my husband's from Shakespeare's *Taming of the Shrew*), or to move to a less demanding job, if his health or happiness makes it desirable.

I find that many women have great problems of communication with their husbands. My limited experience in psychological counseling leads me to believe that this is an area of much of the tension in marriage, and especially in questions of women working. While younger people may have grown up in an era when working wives are the general rule, this is not true of my generation. We women need to be very sensitive to the possibility that a wife who works, and especially one who earns more than her husband, may be a serious threat to his self-esteem. I suspect that there are only two solutions to such a threat. One is for the woman to stop working (or stop earning so much). The second is to work for the kind of communication which makes it possible to talk these things out freely and frankly. This may even require the help of a third party —a clergyman or a counselor.

It is my present expectation that I will retire early and, if it seems wise, take a teaching post for a few years. This would eliminate the need for traveling and leaving my husband alone. It should cut down on the overtime work, and provide long vacations to be together. Since it would also make real use of a hard-won doctorate, it would be a fitting way to end a career.

Thousands of women who are today busy with their homes and children will follow in a pattern like mine. My message to them is—rejoice in the fact that you will have another whole life after your children are grown. It may well be one of the richest and most satisfying parts of your life. Your children will be thankful that you are busy and happy. They will enjoy you more if they don't have to worry about you. Any extra schooling which you can acquire in connection with this second life will be a permanent enrichment. Let's remember to be endlessly grateful for the fact that we are the first generation of women in all of history who have had such an opportunity!

Appendix: The Questionnaire

This questionnaire was sent to respondents who were asked to answer these questions in a personal essay. In the four direct interviews the questionnaire was the basis of the dialogue. Of course, everyone was also free to add comments and expand their answers.

Why do you work? Do your reasons (necessity, other rewards, etc.) affect your attitude to work?

Did you have a life-plan at the beginning of your marriage which included work in addition to child rearing?

Did you, or do you expect to, plan your family size with work or further education in mind?

How many children do you have and how old are they? What different problems with your children at different age levels have you experienced so far as your work is concerned? How have your children responded to your work?

What aspects of your child rearing have given you the greatest concern in pursuing your work?

Have you felt conflict between mothering and working? How have you tried to resolve these conflicts?

What experience have you had with mother-substitutes and nursery schools, so far as small children are concerned? If your children have spent a considerable amount of time in the care of others while you worked, have you worried about the kind of influence these people would have on your children? Have you been especially influenced in your child rearing decisions by any of the literature on women, work, and child rearing?

Were you raised in a family where it was expected that a woman would combine work and child rearing, or in a family which expected that a woman would always remain solely wife and mother? How did these expectations influence you? Do you have any conflict over your lack of leisure, compared to women who do not work?

How do you think our society could be changed or improved to make it easier for women to combine work and mothering?

What kind of work do you do? Do you think that your particular line of work makes it easier or harder to combine family life and work?

From your own experience how would you suggest that young women plan to combine family and work?

What mistakes, if any, do you feel you made in trying to combine family and work? Has your experience taught you things you wish you had known earlier? Do you wish to continue working or would you rather stay at home? Is there any conflict over where "home" should be in regard to work (city?, suburbs?, country?, travel?)?

What conflicts, if any, have you had with your husband concerning your effort to combine mothering and work, or general family life and work? Were you able to resolve these conflicts?

Bibliography

A Consultation on Working Women and Day Care Needs. Washington, D.C., U.S. Department of Labor, 1967.

Allport, Gordon. *Becoming.* New Haven & London: Yale University Press, 1955.

American Women. The Report of the President's Commission on the Status of Women, Edited by Margaret Mead and Frances Balgley Kaplan. New York: Charles Scribner's Sons, Inc., 1965.

Baldwin, Alfred L. *Theories of Child Development.* New York & London: John Wiley & Sons, Inc., 1967.

Bateson, Gregory. "Sex and Culture," in *Personal Character and Cultural Milieu.* Compiled by Douglas C. Haring. Ann Arbor, Michigan: Edwards Brothers, Inc., 1948. Pp. 94-108.

Benedek, Therese. "Some Problems of Motherhood," in *Women: The Variety and Meaning of Their Sexual Experience.* Edited by A. M. Krich. New York: Dell Publishing Co., Inc., 1953.

Benedict, Ruth. "Continuities and Discontinuities in Cultural Conditioning," in *Personality*. Edited by Clyde Kluckhohn and Henry A. Murray. New York: Alfred A. Knopf, Inc., 1948. Pp. 414-423.

Benedict, Ruth. *Patterns of Culture*. Boston, Mass.: Houghton Mifflin Co., 1934, 1959.

Bettelheim, Bruno. *The Empty Fortress*. New York: The Free Press, 1967.

Bettelheim, Bruno. *The Children of the Dream*. New York: The Macmillan Company, 1969.

Beres, David and Obers, Samuel J. "The Effects of Extreme Deprivation in Infancy on Psychic Structure in Adolescence," in *The Psychoanalytic Study of the Child*. Vol. V, 1950. Pp. 212-236. New York: International Universities Press, Inc.

Blood, Robert O. and Hamblin, Robert L. "The Effects of the Wife's Employment on the Family Power Structure," in *The Family*. Edited by Norman W. Bell and Ezra F. Vogel. New York: The Free Press, 1960. Pp. 137-142.

Bowlby, John. *Childcare and the Growth of Love*. Baltimore, Maryland: Penquin Books, 1953.

Bowlby, John. "Some Pathological Processes Engendered by Early Mother-Child Separation," in *Problems of Infancy and Childhood*. Transactions of the Seventh Conference, 1953. New York, New York. Edited by Milton J. E. Senn, Josiah Macy Foundation. Packanack Lake, N. J.: Foundation Press. Pp. 38-89.

Brody, Sylvia. *Passivity*. New York: International Universities Press, Inc., 1964.

Brody, Sylvia. *Patterns of Mothering: Maternal Influence During Infancy*. New York: International Universities Press, 1956.

Bronfenbrenner, Urie. *Two Worlds of Childhood: U.S. and U.S.S.R.* New York: Russell Sage Foundation, 1970.

Caldwell, Bettye M. "The Effects of Infant Care," in *Review of Child Development Research.* Vol. I. New York: Russell Sage Foundation, 1964. Pp. 9-87.

Caplan, Gerald. "Clinical Observations on the Emotional Life of Children in the Communal Settlements in Israel," in *Problems of Infancy and Childhood.* Transactions of the Seventh Conference, 1953. New York, New York. Edited by Milton J. E. Senn, Josiah Macy Foundation. Packanack Lake, N. J.: Foundation Press, Inc.

Children in Collectives. Child-rearing Aims and Practices in the Kibbutz. Edited by Peter B. Neubauer, Springfield, Illinois: Charles C Thomas, 1965.

Coleman, Rose W.; Kris, Ernst; and Provence, Sally. "The Study of Variations of Early Parental Attitudes," in *The Psychoanalytic Study of the Child,* Vol. VIII, 1953. New York: International Universities Press.

Davis, Kingsley. "The Sociology of Parent-Youth Conflict," in *The Adolescent.* Edited by Jerome M. Seidman. New York: The Dryden Press, 1953. Pp. 534-547.

Diamond, Solomon. *Personality and Temperament.* New York: Harper & Row, 1957.

Drucker, Peter F. "Worker and Work in the Metropolis," in *Daedelus.* Fall, 1968, Vol. 97 No. 4. Pp. 1243-1262.

Erikson, Erik. *Childhood and Society,* Second Edition. New York: W. W. Norton & Co., 1963.

Erikson, Erik. *Insight and Responsibility.* New York: W. W. Norton & Co., 1964.

Escalona, Sybille K. "Patterns of Infantile Experiences and the Developmental Process," in *The Psychoanalytic Study of the Child,* Vol. XVIII, 1963, Pp. 197-265.

Fraiberg, Selma. *The Magic Years.* New York: Charles Scribner's Sons, Inc., 1959.

Fraiberg, Selma. "The Origins of Human Bonds," *Commentary*, Vol. 44, December, 1967. P. 55.

Friedan, Betty. *The Feminine Mystique.* New York: W. W. Norton & Co., 1963.

Friedenberg, Edgar Z. *Coming of Age in America.* New York: Random House, 1963.

Freud, Sigmund. *The Ego and the Id.* New York: W. W. Norton & Co., 1960.

Freud, Anna. *The Ego and Mechanisms of Defense.* London: Hogarth, 1937.

Fromm, Erich. "Sex and Character," in *Psychiatry.* Vol. VI, 1943.

Fromm, Erich. *The Sane Society.* New York: Holt, Rinehart & Co., 1955.

Gesell, Arnold Lucius. *The First Five Years of Life.* Yale University Clinic of Child Development. New York: Harper & Brothers, 1940.

Hallowell, A. Irving. "The Child, the Savage, and Human Experience," in *Personal Character and Cultural Milieu.* Edited by Douglas C. Haring. Ann Arbor, Michigan: Edwards Brothers, 1948. Pp. 304-330.

Hartmann, Heinz. *Ego Psychology and the Problem of Adaptation.* New York: International Universities Press, 1958.

Hess, Robert D. "Maternal Teaching Styles and Educational Retardation," *Profile of the School Dropout.* Edited by Daniel Schreiber. New York: Vintage Books, 1968. Pp. 224-234.

Hunt, J. McV. "Experience and the Development of Motivation: Some Reinterpretation," in *Readings in Child Development and Personality.* Edited by Paul H. Mussen, John J. Conger, Jerome Kagan. New York: Harper and Row, 1965.

Isaacs, Mrs. Susan Sutherland. *Social Development in Young Children: A Study of Beginnings.* London: G. Routledge & Sons, 1939.

Kagan, Jerome. "Acquisition and Significance of Sex Typing and Sex Role Identity," in *Review of Child Development Research.* Vol. I. New York: Russell Sage Foundation, 1964. Pp. 137-169.

Kluckhohn, Clyde. *Mirror for Man.* New York: Fawcett World Library, 1967.

Komarovsky, Mirra. *Blue-Collar Marriages.* New York: Vintage Books, 1967.

Komarovsky, Mirra. "Cultural Contradictions and Sex Roles," in *Readings in Sociology.* Edited by Edgar A. Schuler *et al.* New York: Thomas Y. Crowell Co., 1960. Pp. 158-166.

Lewin, Kurt. *Resolving Social Conflicts.* New York: Harper & Brothers, 1948.

Lewin, Kurt. "The Field Theory Approach to Adolescence," in *The Adolescent.* Edited by Jerome M. Seidman. New York: The Dryden Press, 1953. Pp. 32-42.

Lewis, Edwin C. *Developing Woman's Potential.* Amos, Iowa: Iowa State University Press, 1968.

Levy, John and Munroe, Ruth. "The Adolescent and His Happy Family," in *The Adolescent.* Edited by Jerome M. Seidman. New York: The Dryden Press, 1953. Pp. 547-556.

Life Styles of Educated Women. Edited by Jacquelyn A. Mattfeld and Carol G. Van Aken. Cambridge: M.I.T. Press, 1965.

Linton, Ralph. "Concepts of Role and Status," in *Readings*

in Social Psychology. Edited by Theodore M. Newcomb and Eugene L. Hartley. New York: Henry Holt and Company, 1947. Pp. 367-370.

Loevinger, Jane and Sweet, Blanche. "Construction of a Test of Mother's Attitudes," in *Parental Attitudes and Child Behavior.* Edited by John C. Glidewell. Springfield, Illinois: Charles C Thomas, 1960.

Maccoby, Eleanor E. "Effects upon Children of Their Mothers' Outside Employment," in *The Family.* Edited by Norman W. Bell and Ezra F. Vogel. New York: The Free Press, 1960, Pp. 521-538.

Maccoby, Eleanor E. *Woman's Intellect in the Potential of Woman.* Edited by Seymour M. Farber and Roger H. L. Wilson. New York: McGraw-Hill Book Company, Inc., 1963. Pp. 24-37.

McClelland, David. *The Achieving Society.* Princeton, N.J.: Van Nostrand, 1961.

Maslow, Abraham H. *Religions, Values, and Peak-Experiences.* Columbus, Ohio: Ohio State University Press, 1964.

Mead, Margaret. *Male and Female.* New York: William Morrow & Company, Apollo Edition, 1967.

Mead, Margaret. "The Contemporary American Family as an Anthropologist Sees It," in *The Adolescent.* Edited by Jerome M. Seidman. New York: The Dryden Press, 1953. Pp. 524-534.

Merton, Robert K. "Bureaucratic Structure and Personality," in *Personality.* Edited by Clyde Kluckhohn and Henry A. Murray. New York: Alfred A. Knopf. 1948. Pp. 282-291.

Murphy, Lois. "Some Aspects of the First Relationship," *The International Journal of Psychoanalysis.* Vol. 45, 1964.

Myrdal, Alva and Klein, Viola. *Woman's Two Roles: Home and Work.* London: Routledge and Kegan Paul, 1956.

Normal Adolescence. Committee on Adolescence, Group for the Advancement of Psychiatry. New York: Charles Scribner's Sons, Inc., 1968.

Olden, Christine. "Notes on Childbearing in America," in *The Psychoanalytic Study of the Child.* Vol. VII, 1952. Pp. 387-393.

Pappenheim, Else and Sweeney, Mary. "Separation Anxiety in Mother and Child," in *The Psychoanalytic Study of the Child.* Vol. VII, 1952. Pp. 95-115.

Parsons, Talcott. *The Social System.* Glencoe, Illinois: The Free Press, 1951.

Parsons, Talcott. "The Stability of the American Family System," in *The Family.* Edited by Norman Bell and Ezra F. Vogel. Glencoe, Illinois: The Free Press, 1960. Pp. 93-97.

Piaget, Jean. *The Language and Thought of the Child.* Cleveland and New York: Meridian Books, 1955.

Pines, Maya. "Someone to Mind the Baby," *The New York Times Magazine,* January 7, 1968.

Prevention of Mental Disorders in Children. Edited by Gerald Caplan with articles by Brody, Ackerman, Murphy, Pavenstedt, *et al.* New York: Basic Books, Inc., 1961.

Rabban, Meyer. "Sex-Role Identification in Young Children in Two Diverse Social Groups," in *Gen. Psych. Monographs,* 1950, Vol. 42. Pp. 81-158.

Rabin, Albert I. *Growing Up in the Kibbutz.* New York: Springer Publishing Company, Inc., 1965.

Rappaport, David. "The Study of Kibbutz Education and Its Bearing on the Theory of Development," in *The Collected Papers of David Rappaport.* Edited by Merton M. Gill. New York and London: Basic Books, Inc., 1967. Pp. 710-722.

Readings in Child Development & Personality. Edited by Paul H. Mussen, John J. Conger, Jerome Kagan with articles by Anastasi, Bowlby, Harlow, Hunt, Hebb, Piaget, *et al.* New York: Harper & Row, Inc., 1965.

Rheingold, Joseph C. *The Fear of Being a Woman.* New York: Grune & Stratton, 1967.

Sears, Robert R.; Maccoby, Eleanor; and Levin, Harry. *Patterns of Child Rearing.* Evanston, Illinois: Row Peterson and Company, 1957.

Sears, Robert R., Ran Luck, Alpert Richard. *Identification and Childrearing.* Stanford, California: Stanford University Press, 1965.

Sermon, Julia. "Problems of Sex Differences in Space Perception and Aspects of Intellectual Functionings," in *Psychological Review*, June, 1967. Vol. 74 No. 4. Pp. 300-318.

Smuts, Robert W. *Women and Work in America.* New York: Columbia University Press, 1959.

Solley, Charles M. "Affective Processes in Perceptual Development," in *Perceptual Development in Children.* Edited by Allan H. Kidd and Jeanne L. Rivoire. New York: International Universities Press, Inc., 1966.

Spiro, Melford. "Is the Family Universal? The Israeli Case," in *The Family.* Edited by Norman Bell and Ezra F. Vogel, Glencoe, Illinois: The Free Press, 1960, Pp. 64-75.

Spitz, Rene A. "Hospitalism," in *The Psychoanalytic Study of the Child.* New York: International Universities Press, 1946. Vol. II. Pp. 312-342.

Spitz, Rene A. "The Psychogenic Diseases in Infancy," in *The Psychoanalytic Study of the Child.* Vol. 6, 1951. Pp. 255-275.

Sullivan, Harry Stack. *The Collected Works of Harry Stack Sullivan*, Vol. I. New York: W. W. Norton & Co., 1953.

Swift, Joan W. "Effects of Early Group Experience: The Nursery School and Day Nursery," in *Review of Child Development Research.* Vol. I. New York: Russell Sage Foundation, 1964. Pp. 249-288.

The Potential of Women. Edited by Seymour M. Farber and Rober H. L. Wilson. New York: McGraw-Hill Book Company, Inc., 1963.

Theories of Personality. Edited by Calvin S. Hall and Gardner Lindzey. New York: John Wiley & Sons, Inc., 1957.

Tompkins, Silvan Solomon. *Affect, Imagery, Consciousness.* New York: Springer Publishing Co., 1962.

White, Robert W. "Motivation Reconsidered: The Concept of Competence," *Psychological Review,* Vol. 66, 1959. Pp. 297-333.

Witkin, H. A., *et al. Personality Through Perception.* New York: Harper & Row, Inc., 1954.

Wolfenstein, Martha. "Fun Morality: An Analysis of Recent American Childtraining Literature," in *The Psychoanalytic Study of the Child.* Vol. 8, 1953.

Wolfenstein, Martha. "Some Variants in Moral Training of Children," in *The Psychoanalytic Study of the Child.* Vol. V, 1950. Pp. 310-329.

Wolff, Peter. *The Causes, Controls and Organizations of Behavior in the Neonate.* New York: International Universities Press, 1966.

Women and the Scientific Professions: The M.I.T. Symposium on American Women in Science and Engineering. Edited by Jacquelyn A. Mattfeld and Carol G. Van Allen, with papers by Erikson, Bettelheim, Rossi, *et al.* Cambridge: M.I.T. Press, 1965.

Work in the Lives of Married Women. Proceedings of a

Conference on Woman Power. New York: Columbia University Press, 1958.

World Health Organization Study Group on the Psychological Development of the Child. New York: International Universities Press, 1953.